LOST
INVERNESS

*

LOST
INVERNESS

INVERNESS'S LOST
ARCHITECTURAL HERITAGE

*

Norman S. Newton

Norman S. Newton

To Sheila, with grateful thanks for
all your hard work and inspiration for
the local history community in Inverness.

BIRLINN

✳

First published in 2013 by
Birlinn Limited
West Newington House
10 Newington Road
Edinburgh
EH9 1QS

www.birlinn.co.uk

Copyright © Norman S. Newton 2013

ISBN: 978 1 84158 874 2

British Library Cataloguing-in-Publication Data
A catalogue record for this book is available from the British Library

Designed by Mark Blackadder

Typeset in Scotch Roman at Birlinn

Printed and bound by
Gutenberg Press, Malta

CONTENTS

INTRODUCTION

There has been human settlement at the northern end of the Great Glen for at least the last 5,000 years. For most of that long history we have to depend on the slivers and stratifications divined by archaeologists. For the last 1,000 years we have at least the possibility of architectural remains; for the last 500 years we have records and memories of buildings; for the last 100 years we have a richness of reminiscence, memory and photographic record unsurpassed in any other Scottish burgh.

It is essential to grasp the strategic, historical and cultural importance of Inverness's position. The Great Glen, Glen Albyn, is a geological slash through the landscape of the Highlands, linking Argyll and the Atlantic with the Moray Firth and the North Sea, or, as it used to be called, the German Ocean. West of the narrows of the Inner Moray Firth, now crossed by the Kessock Bridge, the Beauly Firth points westwards as a watery finger to the west coast. East of Inverness is fertile, productive farmland, contested by Anglo-Norman and Flemish invaders in the Middle Ages and now eyed covetously by house-developers and speculators. From earliest times, people were lured northwards, across the Black Isle, past the religious magnets of Fortrose, Tain and Dornoch, across the cultural boundary of the Dornoch Firth (the Firth of Tain in early maps), to the Norse northlands of Caithness, Sutherland, Orkney, and eventually Shetland.

It is no surprise that this crossroads in Scotland's physical and cultural landscape was fortified, defended, and fought over for most of its long history. There are well-built and prominent Iron Age hill forts guarding the narrows at Inverness: the Ord Hill overlooking North Kessock on the Black Isle and Craig Phadraig overlooking the town of Inverness. There are persistent traditions associating Macbeth, King of Scotland in the late eleventh century, with Inverness – though not a shred of documentary or physical evidence which would stand up outside the pages of a historical novel. Residents of Auldcastle Road will speak proudly of where Macbeth's castle once stood, undeterred by the lack of any actual architectural or even archaeological proof.

A real stone castle, presumably replacing a timber original, was built as a royal castle during the late middle ages, to solidify royal power in the north. The history of this structure, both real and imagined, has been well documented in Evan Barron's comprehensive book, *Inverness and the Macdonalds* (1930). The MacDonald Lords of the Isles passed through the area on several occasions, sacking and burning the town routinely, most noticeably on their way to the inconclusive battle at Harlaw in 1411.

The final battle for Inverness, at least in the military sense, took place on 16 April 1746, when an army of Highland clansmen, Frenchmen, Lowlanders and a few Irish were comprehensively defeated by the professional Hanoverian army of battle-hardened regiments, including many Lowland and Highland Scots. We call this the Battle of Culloden, but even a cursory visit to the battlefield and its excellent National Trust for Scotland interpretative centre makes it abundantly clear that this was a battle for control of the Highland capital. The vicious aftermath of Culloden certainly made it clear to the local population, many of whom turned out on the day as sightseers, that the government saw control of Inverness, and therefore of the whole Scottish Highlands, as a matter of urgent priority.

The real damage done by Culloden was not the carnage on the battlefield, unremitting as that was, or even the brutality of the days and weeks following, but the decades of cultural suppression and economic exploitation which followed.

Twenty years after Inverness celebrated (as many did) the centenary of Culloden, the town embarked on a period of redevelopment which saw the almost total obliteration of any pre-nineteenth century buildings. Nobody could emulate the Victorians for focused ruthlessness, whether on colonial battlefields or in urban redevelopment. The irony that their unrivalled in quality urban architecture itself came under equally ruthless threat a hundred years later, in the 1960s, is not lost on modern researchers.

So, leaving aside the numerous episodes of pillage and destruction in the middle ages, Inverness has gone through two serious periods of systematic destruction of its architectural heritage: firstly in response to the Railway Age, when a group of young professionals completely redesigned the town centre, to their own immense gain; and secondly, in the 1960s and 1970s, when excruciatingly bad concrete boxes – and car parks – replaced, depressingly, far too many Victorian buildings.

In this book, we shall look in some detail at over 100 lost buildings. Those lost in the twentieth century, and in the last decade of the nineteenth century, are often preserved in old photographs; the handful of earlier structures of which we have any real knowledge survive only in a few engravings and in some old maps. Of the buildings lost in the twentieth century, many went within living memory and survive not only on photographs but also in the recollections of the local population. Recognising that none of us is getting any younger and that one way of fighting back against the predations of property developers is to record memories of our lost cultural heritage, the Inverness Remembered group, under the umbrella of the Inverness Local History Forum, has, since 1992, recorded and transcribed many hundreds of hours of memories, often from very elderly informants. They have published edited extracts and highlights of these reminiscences and mounted exhibitions of photographic material, much of it contributed by local people. The Inverness Local History Forum also organises lectures on Inverness history and publishes a Newsletter.

Another organisation, the Inverness Field Club, also campaigns to preserve the architectural heritage of Inverness and has featured some aspects of the architectural history of the town in some of its publications. The Inverness Civic Trust campaigns on behalf of the remaining historic townscape, resisting demolitions of surviving historic buildings.

ACKNOWLEDGEMENTS

Many thanks to the staff in the Reference Room at Inverness Public Library, to the staff of the Am Baile website and of the Highland Photographic Archive, and to the staff at the Highland Archive Service. It is always a pleasure to pay tribute to former colleagues. A mixture of thanks and apologies to the editors at Birlinn, whose patience was sorely tested but whose professionalism triumphed in the end.

There are probably more people today in Inverness with an interest in the past – and the future – of their town than at any point in the past. Members of the Inverness Civic Trust, Inverness Field Club, Inverness Local History Forum and the Highland Family History Society have all provided support and encouragement.

Lastly, thanks to all those Invernessians who racked their ageing memories for the trivia which brings historical research to life; some of what you told me is probably libellous and unrepeatable, but certainly informed my approach!

CHAPTER 1

INVERNESS IN HISTORY

Where did the earliest inhabitants of Inverness live? The flat ground occupied by the modern town was probably unsuited for prehistoric settlement; recent archaeological excavations tend to support the view that the earliest settlements were on the slopes overlooking the valley bottom. Occasional finds point to burials and other human activity on low-lying ground, but it seems clear that in the Iron Age the main focus of settlement was the hill fort on Craig Phadraig, with presumably farms on the surrounding slopes.

The only other prehistoric structure to survive is the probable Neolithic kerb cairn now located on the Raigmore housing estate, behind Raigmore Hospital. It is not, however, in its original position; it would have been obliterated by the A9, and after excavation it was moved to its present location.

In Inverness Museum, on Bridge Street, can be found much of the archaeological material found over the years in and around Inverness. The Highland Council's archaeologists maintain a database of information on archaeological sites and find spots, the Highland Historic Environment Record.

THE PICTS

We know very little about the people who occupied the Iron Age fort on Craig Phadraig, but quite a lot about the folk who occupied the site towards the end of its life – the Picts. Excavations on Craig Phadraig in the 1970s revealed disappointingly little evidence, and certainly not nearly enough to claim it as a Pictish 'Dark Age' fort. We know that there was a Pictish fort at Inverness – it was visited by St Columba of Iona around 582AD. An account of Columba's interaction with local druids and with King Brude of the Picts, along with an exciting early account of 'Nessie', survives in Adomnan's biography – or hagiography – of Columba. There is, of course, absolutely no detail of any buildings or structures.

A more likely candidate for Brude's fort is perhaps Torvean, near the swing bridge carrying the A82 over the Caledonian Canal on the way to Loch

Ness and the Great Glen. The name refers to an early Christian saint, St Bean; at the base of the hill, on the flat ground between there and Tomnahurich Hill, Pictish graves were found when Tomnahurich Cemetery was extended, and in 1807, during the construction of the Caledonian Canal, a magnificent Pictish silver chain, now in the National Museum of Scotland in Edinburgh, was discovered. These chains, of which only a very few examples are known, are thought to have belonged to important Pictish rulers or high-ranking officials.

Torvean Hill has been much disturbed by quarrying and it is unlikely that this debate will ever be definitively resolved.

THE MIDDLE AGES

We know very little about the townscape of Inverness in the medieval period. We know there was a town there, but we are not really very sure of its size or extent. Archaeological excavations in the 1970s seemed to show that the medieval town, bounded by a fosse or ditch, was not as large as had been previously thought.

The eastern line of the town ditch seems to have followed the line of what is now Academy Street, and Hamilton Street, at the western edge of the Eastgate shopping centre. It used to be thought that it ran along the edge of the Barnhill (Ardconnel Street), but excavations on Castle Street in the 1970s seemed to show that there was no development there until the middle of the thirteenth century, making a defensive ditch on the Barnhill unnecessary. On the west side of the river there is unlikely to have been any medieval occupation before the thirteenth century, when a bridge is first recorded. Thereafter the boundary was marked by the line of what is now King Street and Alexander Place. According to records from the reign of William the Lion (1143–1214), the state bore the responsibility of making the ditch, but the burgesses of Inverness were responsible for its upkeep, and for making and maintaining a palisade along its line.

The thirteenth century buildings on Castle Street were very ordinary houses and workshops of plank and clay wall construction, but were succeeded in the fourteenth century by more substantial timber buildings. It was during the middle ages, in the years between 1100 and 1600, that Inverness became an important centre of trade and settlement. It was primarily the strategic position of the town which was the determining factor in its growth, but without formal authorisation from central government, in the form of official Charters from the Kings (and Queens) of Scotland, the burgh of Inverness could not have flourished in the way it did.

Even so, it was not until the last quarter of the nineteenth century, with the arrival of the railway, that it became clear that Inverness, rather than, for example, Cromarty, or Dingwall, or Elgin, was going to become the main trading port and administrative centre in the north of Scotland.

The dominant buildings of medieval Inverness were the Castle, of which nothing survives, and, at the other end of Church Street, the parish church, parts of which survive in the tower of the later structure now on the site. This street plan for a medieval burgh was very common, with church and state providing the major axis of the town.

There are persistent traditions in Inverness that Macbeth, who succeeded to the throne of Scotland in 1040, had a castle in Inverness. Victorian antiquarians were keen on a site on Auldcastle Road, on top of ancient cliffs overlooking Eastgate, but no definitive evidence has ever been found. There is a King Duncan's well on the edge of the Raigmore estate, with plaques unsubstantiated by any historical evidence. If Macbeth did have a castle in Inverness it would probably have been a wooden structure, on an artificial mound or motte, defended by a wooden palisade – there is an excellent example at Lumphanan in Aberdeenshire, where Macbeth was killed in 1057. There are no traces of anything like this on Auldcastle Road. If there was an eleventh-century castle in Inverness, it is far more likely that it was built on the Castle Hill, guarding the crossing point of the Ness. It seems likely that the present mound, on which a stone castle was built in the twelfth century, is, at least in part, artificial. The stone castle is likely to have been built in the reign of David I, if experience in other parts of Scotland is anything to go by.

Fortunately we do have surviving engravings of the stone castle, which, after more centuries of expansion and improvement, was blown up by the Jacobites in 1746 and comprehensively demolished, without any surviving trace, in the 1830s, when the courthouse and prison which now occupy the Castle Hill were built.

Although well outside the boundaries of the Royal Burgh, there is another medieval castle in the district, also completely gone, but with surviving contemporary illustrations. This is the castle variously known as Castle Bona, or Bona Castle, or Caisteal Spioradain, located between Lochend and Dochfour, at the north end of Loch Ness, just north of the Bona lighthouse. Only the faintest traces of a mound survive – the stonework was demolished and used by the builders of the Caledonian Canal.

The Castle takes its name from the 'spirits' or ghosts of prisoners who were massacred there during the centuries of clan warfare. It is likely that the victims were Camerons and the perpetrators were the local Macleans

Castle Spirden   Bona Ferry   Aldaurie   Lochness & the Stratherick Hills & part of Urquhart

The seat of the Baillies since 1452   Alexander Baillie of Dunain married Anne the youngest daughter of
Sir Archibald Campbell of Clunes, by Anne the only child of Macpherson of Clunie.   Dochfour a branch of Dunain.

Top: Castle Bona. Bottom: Dochfour House. Both watercolours from the book The
Ancient and Honourable Family of Calder.

of Dochgarroch. The Macleans of Urquhart had been raiding in Cameron country, at the south end of the Great Glen, and had brought booty and hostages back to their own area, eventually occupying the stronghold at Bona. The Camerons launched a retaliatory raid, capturing two of Maclean's sons and offering to exchange hostages. Maclean carried out his threat to kill all his captives unless the Camerons withdrew; the Camerons then killed their Maclean prisoners, and a pitched battle ensued, which the Macleans won. It is thought that these events took place around 1450. Maclean clan histories illustrate the sometimes violent and cruel nature of clan society. The castle mound, and a substantial stone keep, are illustrated in watercolours thought to date from around 1810 contained in *The Ancient and Honourable Family of Calder*, in the Fraser-Mackintosh Collection at Inverness Library.

The only other 'outlier' covered in this book is Culloden House, once far out in the country but arguably now contained within the eastern suburbs of Inverness, lying between Smithton and Balloch, surrounded by housing developments. The current house, now an excellent country house hotel, dates from the 1780s, but replaces an earlier seventeenth century fortified house, perhaps built by Mackintoshes. By 1745 it was in possession of Duncan Forbes of Culloden, Lord President of the Court of Session and ardent Hanoverian. Bonnie Prince Charlie stayed there before the fateful battle of Culloden in

Culloden House, from an engraving in Keltie's A History of the Scottish Highlands, Highland Clans and Highland Regiments *(1874)*.

April 1746, though not in any of the existing bedrooms – the house he stayed in was destroyed by fire around 1780, except for what is now the basement.

The illustration of the original house (previous page) is an engraving in Keltie's *A History of the Scottish Highlands, Highland Clans and Highland Regiments* (1874), from an 'original sketch' in possession of Duncan Forbes of Culloden. It shows the house which burned down in the 1780s, to be replaced by the present house, now a hotel.

After the battle of Culloden Bonnie Prince Charlie's victorious cousin, the Duke of Cumberland, also stayed there. Its owner, Duncan Forbes of Culloden, was away at the time. As an avid supporter of the Hanoverian cause, he had invested his own money in ensuring the loyalty of some Highland clans. At the Hanoverian court in London, he fell out of favour with the king by pleading for clemency and leniency for some Jacobite prisoners – a course of action which ruined him financially, as the government never repaid the money he had spent in the Hanoverian cause.

The current Georgian mansion, much altered but with some original internal features, was built on the same site and incorporates in its basement some features of the older house. It is clear that the approaches to the house today, including the sweeping drive, are not the original ground level. There are gun-ports in some of the basement windows, now well below ground level, and the current entrance leads up steps to what would have been the first floor level of the original building.

It is perhaps worth taking a moment to consider the bridges of Inverness – Timothy Pont's manuscript maps of the 1590s are the earliest depiction of a stone bridge at the natural crossing point of the Ness, below the Castle Hill. A stone bridge of seven arches, probably built in the late seventeenth century, was swept away in a great flood in 1849 and replaced by the late, lamented Suspension Bridge between 1852 and 1855. Today's bridge, planned before World War II, was finally opened in 1961. The knock-on effects included the widening of Bridge Street to accommodate increased traffic flow and then the subsequent demolitions of many much-loved buildings.

In 1899, Alexander Mackenzie published *The Prophecies of the Brahan Seer*, in which it is predicted that when the ninth bridge over the Ness was completed, "the Highlands will be overrun by ministers without grace and women without shame." In his commentary, Mackenzie opined that this was "a prediction which some maintain has all the appearance of being rapidly fulfilled at this moment." Perhaps we are now safe: at the last count, the replacement railway bridge constructed in 1990 is the twentieth bridge to span the Ness.

From time to time local campaigners espouse the cause of 'Cromwell's Tower', located north of the town centre on the site of the fort built during the Civil War of the 1650s. Recent research has proved beyond any doubt that the surviving clock tower is part of the offices of a rope factory, dating from the 1780s. It does not appear in any seventeenth or eighteenth-century plans or drawings of the 'Old Fort'.

It is perhaps worth closing this section by remarking that when it comes to demolished architectural treasures, Inverness will never be in the same league as Aberdeen, Dundee, Glasgow or Edinburgh. Despite its current pretensions, Inverness was, and some would say always will be, a small Scottish provincial burgh, which has done quite well for itself but on a much more modest scale than its metropolitan competitors. The population did not exceed 20,000 until 1900 and did not pass 30,000 until the 1960s. Since then the population has doubled in 50 years and now just surpasses 60,000. Outside of the compact town centre there are few buildings of note, historic or contemporary. The Victorians did their usually thorough job in sweeping away almost all earlier buildings, so the total losses, although keenly felt by native Invernessians with memories of the excesses of the 1960s, are nothing on the scale of the losses in other Scottish cities.

Having said that, there is undoubtedly still the need for a comprehensive architectural history of Inverness, including all the buildings which escaped demolition, and it is to be hoped that one of our thriving professional architectural community will be able to undertake this task.

CHAPTER 2

EARLY VIEWS OF INVERNESS

INVERNESS 1585-95

Probably the earliest 'views' of Inverness appear on the manuscript maps of Timothy Pont, a young graduate of St Andrew's University, who in the 1580s and 1590s walked around the whole of the mainland and islands of Scotland, collecting material for a projected county atlas of Scotland. The published atlas did not appear until 1654, when engravings based on Pont's surveys were produced by the Amsterdam mapmaker Blaeu.

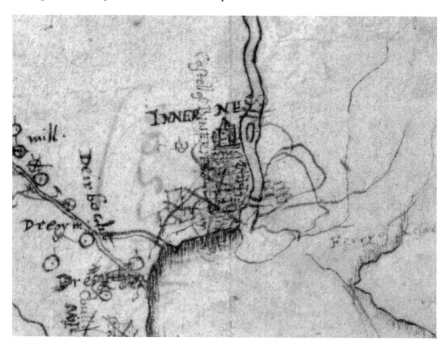

This detail from the sheet known as 'Pont 8' shows the fifteenth-century stone castle clearly, two bridges over the Ness and the Ness Islands, but for some reason Pont crossed out his sketchy drawing of the town. With the eye of faith it might just be possible to make out the Old High Church. This admittedly very scrappy 'map' also shows the 'Ferry of Kesack' and the settlement of 'Deirbocht' (Dirriebught). There are just a few buildings shown on the west side of the river.

Inverness also appears on 'Pont 5': in this version there is a better rendition of the bridge and at the mouth of the river is a structure which might possibly be an early beacon or lighthouse.

As well as 'Innernesse', other places named on this Pont map are Markinch, Balefair (Ballifeary), Kilmailie (Kinmylies), Dunenmoir, Dunenchroy, Lagnalien, Dochafour, Docharn and the Castle of Borlam (Borlum). The Ness Islands are clearly shown. The map may be crude, but the information is good.

The Blaeu atlas published in 1654 is prettier, but the information on Pont's manuscripts is fifty years older, and more immediate, despite its scrappy appearance. All of the surviving Pont maps are in the National Library of Scotland, and available online through their website. The images can be enlarged and manipulated to improve legibility, and have proved to be an invaluable source for the study of Scottish history. Pont was not a Gaelic speaker, as far as we know, but had a good ear. His almost phonetic renditions of place names sometimes provide us with a unique insight into their meanings.

Pont's drawings of important buildings are not just schematic or symbolic versions, but in many cases have been shown to be accurate architectural drawings. There are almost limitless opportunities for further research.

It has been noted, for example, that his sketches of mountain profiles are often readily identifiable and can assist in working out his itinerary around the Highlands.

INVERNESS IN 1693

Slezer's view of Inverness (1693).

One hundred years after Pont's maps, a famous view of Inverness appeared as an engraving in John Slezer's *Theatrum Scotiae* (1693). Slezer was a native of Holland who settled in Scotland in 1669. His book of views of Scottish towns and cities, with text by Sir Robert Sibbald, is one of the few primary sources for information on seventeenth-century Scottish architecture.

A version of Slezer's engraving appeared in Charles Fraser-Mackintosh's *Invernessiana* (1875). Prominent buildings include the Old High Church, St Columba's, and the Castle, still awaiting destruction by the Jacobites in 1746. The original version has been digitised by the National Library of Scotland and appears on its website, allowing the possibility of zooming in to the detail of individual buildings.

There are three substantial ships at the harbour (opposite, top), testifying to the importance of Inverness as a trading port. The buildings beyond the harbour, at least one of them in ruins, are presumably the remains of the Civil War fort.

In another part of Slezer's view of Inverness (opposite, bottom),

Top and bottom: details from Slezer's view of Inverness.

presumably almost none of the buildings survive, except for the Old High Church and Dunbar's Hospital, on Church Street.

In the detail above, the Town Steeple is prominent, and the arches of the stone bridge are clearly visible. The impressive castle was blown up by the Jacobites in 1746 and subsequently completely cleared and demolished to make way for the new courthouse in 1832 and the new prison in 1835.

INVERNESS IN 1725

View of Inverness in 1725 from a map of the period.

After the Jacobite rising of 1715, Inverness was occupied by the British Army and the castle became a garrison. General Wade, followed by Major Caulfeild (whose surname is mis-spelled in many roads and streets around his house of Cradlehall), busied themselves building many hundreds of miles of roads and bridges, linking army forts and barracks strategically placed around the Highlands.

Above: details from the 1725 map.

Along the top of a map of the area dating from this time is a view of the Inverness skyline in 1725, drawn for the Board of Ordnance – which eventually became the Ordnance Survey of Great Britain. It can be viewed on the website of the National Library of Scotland, with zoom facilities which allow a closer look at some of the detail. The seven arches of the stone bridge, with the gatehouses guarding each end of the bridge, are shown clearly.

INVERNESS IN 1776

An engraving of Inverness in the 1770s is to be found in Thomas Pennant's *Tour of Scotland* (1776). Viewed from Island Bank Road, the Ness Islands are on the left. St Columba's Church, the stone bridge and the Castle are prominent.

Along with Boswell and Johnson, Pennant was one of the first 'tourists' to visit the Highlands. A Welshman, he did not complain about the terrain in the way that the rather portly Englishman and his Scottish gentry companion did. Pennant's descriptions of his travels are important in the social history of the Highlands, though sadly he was not too impressed with the town of Inverness and gives a very minimal account of its townscape.

INVERNESS IN 1791

Boswell, Johnson and Pennant paved the way for an increasing torrent of visitors, attracted by the sublime, romantic landscape, further popularised by the Lakeland poets. A typical engraving of Inverness, viewed from high ground above Island Bank Road, is from Thomas Newte's *Prospects and Observations on a Tour of England and Scotland* (1791). Prominent is the stone bridge, destroyed by a flood in 1849. The Castle is in ruins, blown up by the retreating Jacobites in 1746, a couple of months before the disaster at Culloden. Two spires are visible: the Old High Church, beside the river, and the spire of the Tolbooth, just above the horse and cart. There are solidly built stone buildings in the town, and a few buildings on the west side of the river, including the well-built toll-gathering structure known also from later sources. Down at the harbour, near where the River Ness joins the Beauly

Engraving of Inverness from Thomas Newte's Prospects and Observations on a Tour of England and Scotland *(1791)*.

Firth, are industrial buildings, including perhaps the long buildings of the rope work which was built on the site of Cromwell's fort of the 1650s.

INVERNESS IN 1821

John Wood was a prolific cartographer, who made plans of most Scottish towns in the 1820s. His town plan of Inverness in 1821 (next page) may not show any architectural elevations, but it is a detailed map of the town before the mid-Victorian improvements. The most important buildings are numbered and a key at the side of the map identifies some the owners, as follows:

1. English Chapel (Old High Church)
2. Gaelic Parish Church (Church St)
3. Episcopalian Church (Church St)
4. Chapel of Ease (Margaret St)
5. Roman Catholic Chapel (Margaret St)
6. Tax Office and Town Clerk's Office (Church St)
7. Perth Bank (corner of Church St and Fraser's Lane)
8. Independent Meeting House (Bank Street)

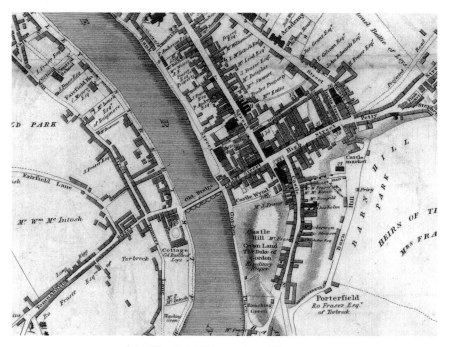

John Wood's 1821 town plan of Inverness.

9. House of Lady Drummuir where Prince Charles and the Duke of Cumberland lodged in 1746 (Church St – Abertarff House)
10. Custom House (Church St)
11. Crown Hotel Mr Robertson (Church St)
12. Mason Lodge Hotel Mr Bennet (Church St)
13. Secession Church (Baron Taylor's St)
14. Bank of Scotland (Bank St)
15. Northern Meeting Rooms (Church St)
16. Methodist Chapel (Inglis St)
17. Theatre (Inglis St)
18. Queen Mary's House James Robertson Esquire's Property (Bridge St)
19. Jail (corner of Church St and High St)
20. Atheneum (corner of Church St and High St)
21. British Linen Company's Bank (High St)
22. Starr Inn Mr Geddes (Castle Wynd)
23. Town Hall and Clach na Cuddan (Bridge St)
24. Courier Office (High St)
25. Fish Meal and Green Market (High St)
26. Inverness Journal Office (Petty St)

27. Raining's Charity School (top of Raining's Stairs)
28. Sheriff Clerk's Office (Castle St)
1.1. Old Meal Market Lane (connecting High St to Baron Taylor's St)
2.2. Grant's Lane (as above)
3.3. Cumming Lane (as above)
4.4 King's Baker Lane (as above)

This plan is the first detailed attempt to identify the important buildings of Inverness, and since it predates the first edition of the Ordnance Survey, which came to Inverness in the 1860s, it is an important record of the town before the mid-Victorian 'improvers' swept away most of the old buildings in the town centre. There is a copy of John Wood's map in the new Highland Archive and Registration Centre (HARC), which opened its premises to the general public in 2010 at its site beside the Bught Park. It can also be viewed in detail online at the National Library of Scotland digital map library.

CHAPTER 3

BURT'S LETTERS

The starting point for any study of the architectural history of Inverness has to be the accounts written by Captain Edmund Burt, an army officer who was stationed in Inverness during the period of military road building in the 1730s. He had dealings with the famous road-builder, General George Wade, commander-in-chief of the British Army in Scotland, though was not directly involved in that enterprise. It seems that in 1725 he was appointed to a post with responsibility for collecting rents from unsold forfeited estates in the Highlands, following the Jacobite rising in 1715. One of the few unsold estates was Glenmoriston, so in the *Letters* there are quite a few accounts of travelling in the Great Glen. Addressed to a friend in England, his letters, apparently written in 1727 and 1728, though not published until 1754, contain many interesting glimpses into town life, few of them flattering. These passages describe the condition of ordinary people:

> Here is a melancholy appearance of objects in the streets; – in one part the poor women, maid-servants, and children, in the coldest weather, in the dirt or in snow, either walking or standing to talk to one another without stockings or shoes. In another place, you see a man dragging along a half-starved horse little bigger than an ass, in a cart, about the size of a wheel-barrow . . . Some of these carts are led by women, who are generally bare-foot, with a blanket for the covering of their bodies, and in cold or wet weather they bring it quite up over them . . . How miserable would be the children of the poor that one sees continually in the streets! Their wretched food makes them look pot-bellied; they are seldom washed . . . boys have nothing but a coarse kind of vest buttoned down the back . . . girls have a piece of blanket wrapped about their shoulders, and are bareheaded like the boys; and both without stockings and shoes in the hardest of the seasons.

Burt's *Letters from a Gentleman in the North of Scotland to his Friend in London* contains some of the earliest detailed descriptions of the Inverness townscape. It also contains the first town plan of Inverness, albeit covering only the centre of the town, with the Castle and the bridge prominent.

Burt has many descriptions of the details of buildings, but he starts with this general description of the town and its castle:

> The Town principally consists of four Streets, of which three centre at the Cross, and the other is something irregular.

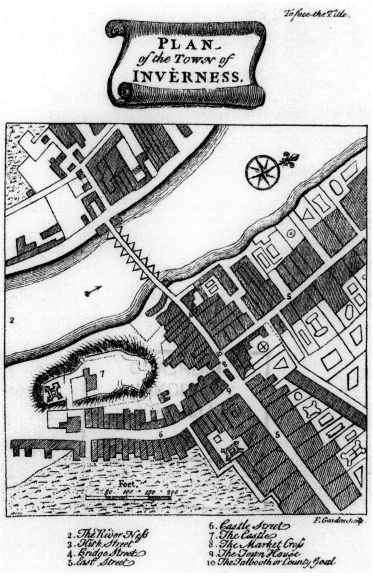

Burt's plan of Inverness.

Inverness Castle and the stone bridge.

The Castle stands upon a little steep Hill closely adjoining to the Town, on the South Side, built with unhewn Stone; it was lately in Ruins, but is now completely repaired, to serve as a Part of the Citadel of Fort George, whereof the first Foundation Stone was laid in Summer 1726, and is to consist of Barracks for six Companies. This Castle, whereof the Duke of Gordon is hereditary Keeper, was formerly a Royal Palace, where Mary, the mother of our King James the First, resided, at such Times when she thought it her Interest to oblige the Highlanders with her Presence and Expense, or that her Safety required it.

You will think it was a very scanty Palace, when I have told you, that before it was repaired, it consisted of only six Lodging-

Rooms, the Offices below, and the Gallery above; which last being taken down, and the Rooms divided each into two, there are now twelve Apartments for Officers' Lodgings.

Burt was impressed by the stone bridge, though not by attempts to circumvent paying the toll for its use:

> The Bridge is about eighty Yards over, and a Piece of Good Workmanship, consisting of seven Arches, built with Stone, and maintained by a Toll of a Bodle or the sixth Part of a Penny for each foot-passenger with Goods; a Penny for a loaded Horse, &c.
>
> And here I cannot forbear to give you an Instance of the extreme Indigence of some of the Country People, by assuring you, I have seen Women with heavy Loads, at a Distance from the Bridge (the Water being low), wade over the large Stones, which are made slippery by the Sulphur, almost up to the Middle, at the Hazard of their Lives, being desirous to save, or unable to pay, one single bodle.

He was also impressed by the sight of local 'wenches' washing clothes in the river beside the bridge, by stamping on the clothes in tubs, with bare feet and legs bright red from the cold water. The 'stone of the tubs', Clachnacuddin, is thus the iconic symbol of Inverness and now stands at the entrance to the Town House, beside the Mercat Cross. Burt describes the old Town House and the adjacent area:

> The Town-Hall is a plain Building of Rubble; and there is one Room in it, where the Magistrates meet upon the Town Business, which would be tolerably handsome, but the Walls are rough, not whitewashed, or so much as plastered; and no Furniture in it but a Table, some bad Chairs, and altogether immoderately dirty.
>
> The Market-Cross is the Exchange of the Merchants, and other Men of Business.
>
> There they stand in the Middle of the dirty Street, and are frequently interrupted in their Negociations by Horses and Carts, which often separate them one from another in the Midst of their Bargains or other Affairs. But this is nothing extraordinary in Scotland; for it is the same in other Towns, and even at the Cross of Edinburgh.
>
> Over-against the Cross is the Coffee-House. A Gentleman, who loves Company and Play, keeps it for his Diversion; for so I am told

The 'wenches' washing clothes.

by the People of the Town; but he has condescended to complain to me of the little he gets by his Countrymen.

As to a Description of the Coffee-Room, the Furniture, and Utensils, I must be excused in that particular, for it would not be a very decent one; but I shall venture to tell you in general that the Room appears as if it had never been cleaned since the Building of the House; and, in Frost and Snow, you might cover the Peat-Fire with your Hands.

He found the terminology and language of architecture very different to what he was used to:

By the Way, they call a Floor a House; the Whole Building is called a Land; an Alley, as I said before, is a *Wynde*; a little Court, or a turn-again Alley, is a *Closs*; a round Stair-case, a *Turnpike*; and a square one goes by the name of a *Skale Stair*. In this Town the Houses are so differently modelled, they cannot be brought under any general Description; but commonly the back Part, or one End, is turned toward the Street, and you pass by it through a short Alley into a little Court-Yard, to ascend by Stairs above the first Story. This lowest Stage of the Building has a Door toward the Street, and serves for a Shop or a Warehouse, but has no Communication with the rest.

Highlanders at the Mercat Cross.

Burt goes on to describe in some detail the construction methods used:

The Houses are for the most part low, because of the violent Flur-
ries of Wind which often pour upon the Town from the Openings of
the adjacent Mountains, and are built with Rubble-Stone, as are all
the Houses in every other Town of Scotland that I have seen, except
Edinburgh, Glasgow, Perth, Stirling, and Aberdeen; where some of
them are faced with Ashler Stone; but the four Streets of Glasgow,
as I have said before, are so from one end to the other.

The Rubble Walls of these Houses are composed of Stones of
different Shapes and Sizes; and many of them, being Pebbles, are
almost round, which, in laying them, leave large Gaps, and on the
outside they fill up those Interstices by driving in flat Stones of
a small Size; and, in the end, face the Work all over with Mortar
thrown against it with a Trowel, which they call harling.

This Rough-Casting is apt to be damaged by the Weather, and
must be sometimes renewed, otherwise some of the Stones will drop
out.

The Chasms in the Inside and Middle of these Walls, and the dis-
proportionate Quantity of Mortar, by Comparison, with the Stone,
render them receptacles for prodigious numbers of Rats, which
scratch their way from the Inside of the House half through the Wall,
where they burrow and breed securely, and by that means abound
every where in the small Scots Towns, especially near the Sea.

The Houses of this Town were neither sashed nor slated before
the Union, as I have been informed by several old People: and to this
day the Ceilings are rarely Plastered: nothing but the single Boards
serve for Floor and Ceiling, and the partitions being often composed
of upright Boards only, they are sometimes shrunk, and any body
may not only hear, but see, what passes in the room adjoining.

Those Houses that are not sashed, have two Shutters that turn
upon Hinges for the low half of the Window, and only the upper Part
is glazed; so that there is no seeing any Thing in the Street, in Bad
Weather, without great inconvenience.

Burt found these window arrangements curious, and was unconvinced
with the explanation:

Asking the reason of this, I was told that these People still continue those Shutters as an old Custom which was at first occasioned by Danger; for that formerly, in their Clan-Quarrels, several had been shot from the opposite Side of the Way, when they were in their Chamber, and by these Shutters they were concealed and in safety; but I believe the true reason is, the saving the expense of Glass, for it is the same in the out-parts of all the Towns and Cities in the Low Country.

He also noticed the less salubrious houses:

What I have hitherto said, with Respect to the Buildings of this Town, relates only to the principal Part of the Streets; the middling

Highlanders in Highland scenery.

Sort of Houses, as in other Towns, are very low, and have generally a close Wooden-Stair Case before the front. By one end of this
you ascend, and in it above are small round or oval Holes, just big
enough for the Head to go through; and in Summer, or when any
Thing extraordinary happens in the Street to excite the Curiosity
of the Inhabitants, they look like so many People with their Heads
in the Pillory.

But the extreme Parts of the Town are made up of most miser-
ably low, dirty Hovels, faced and covered with Turf, with a bottom-
less Tub, or Basket, in the Roof for a Chimney.

Burt was critical not just of personal hygiene, but also of municipal
responsibilities:

The Pavement here is very good; but, as in other small Towns where
the Streets are narrow, it is so much rounded, that when it is dry, it
is dangerous to ride, insomuch that Horses which are shod are often
falling; and when it is dirty, and beginning to dry, it is slippery to the
Feet, for in Scotland you walk generally in the Middle of the Streets.

I asked the Magistrates one Day, when the Dirt was almost
above one's Shoes, why they suffered the Town to be so excessively
dirty, and did not employ People to cleanse the Street? The Answer
was, "It will not be long before we have a Shower."

The Lodgings of the ordinary People are indeed most miserable
ones; and even those of some who make a tolerable Appearance in
the Streets are not much better.

His description of Cromwell's Fort is interesting:

I shall begin with the Ruins of a Fort built by Oliver Cromwell in
the Year 1653 or 1654, which, in his Time, commanded the Town,
the Mouth of the River, and Part of the Country on the Land Sides
of it where there are no hills. It lies something to the North-East of
us, and is washed by a navigable Part of the Ness, near its Issue in
to the Murray Frith.

The Figure of the Out-work is a Pentagon of two hundred Yards
to a Side, surrounded to Landward with a Fosse, now almost filled
up with Rubbish. The Rampart is not unpleasant for a Walk in a
Summer's Evening.

Oliver had 1,200 Men in and near this Citadel, under the Command of one Colonel Fitz, who had been a Tailor, as I have been informed by a very ancient Laird, who said he remembered every remarkable Passage which happened at that Time, and, most especially Oliver's Colours, which were so strongly impressed on his Memory, that he thought he then saw them spread out by the Wind, with the Word Emmanuel (God with us) upon them, in very large golden Characters.

Near the Fort is the Quay, where there are seldom more than two or three Ships, and those of no great Burden.

Burt died in London in 1755. The *Letters* are an important source for the social history of Inverness and the Highlands, and deserve to be more widely known and studied. They were reprinted in the 1970s, and are available in an edition published by Birlinn in most libraries.

CHAPTER 4

SOURCES

Other sources for the history of the buildings and architecture of Inverness are sparse, but what survives can, with local knowledge, become interesting and revealing and shed light on the current townscape. The ultimate encyclopaedia of the buildings of Inverness remains to be written. John Gifford has provided an excellent inventory of surviving structures in his *Highlands and Islands* volume in the Penguin Buildings of Scotland series (1992), but of course what is lacking in that survey are the people who occupied the buildings he described. In *Lost Inverness* we are considering only the missing buildings, those demolished, burnt down and abandoned, and even then we are constrained by the availability of suitable illustrations to record what is now a fading memory for surviving Invernessians.

There must be many structures which have disappeared without trace, without memory. Large-scale Ordnance Survey maps from the nineteenth century may show structures of which there is now no trace and no written or photographic record. It also has to be said that photographs showing only rather boring, featureless back closes would be of limited interest, even to architectural aficionados.

Because surviving accounts of Inverness are so very few, it seems reasonable to quote what there is quite extensively – bearing in mind that these extracts are from writings which also include lots of other material relating to the social history of Inverness.

In his *Memorabilia of Inverness*, which appeared in the *Inverness Courier* in 1822 and was republished in a small book in 1887, James Sutor collected together some interesting snippets from the minutes of the Town Council and other sources. He was born around 1795, dying in 1869 at the age of 74.

He notes that in 1697 some of the streets were 'newly paved', that in 1738 'the most extensive part of the harbour, commonly called the New Quay or Citadel Quay, was built' and that in 1746, after the Battle of Culloden, 'By a note in the town's records it would appear that the streets were this year swept at the public expense for the first time by command of the Duke of Cumberland'. The Town Hall was enlarged and improved in 1750, at public expense, and in 1761 he notes: 'an attempt made to have the streets regularly swept, by setting the street manure on lease'. In 1768 'embankment of the town's lands at the Longman' was extended, at a cost of £100 from public funds – 'before this time the sea flowed over most of the lands lying to the east and south east of Cromwell's fort'. The Chapel Yard was enclosed by a stone wall, paid for by the Burgh, in 1771.

In 1777 Sutor says that 'the principal inhabitants subscribed to buy fire engines. The reason given in the preamble of the subscription paper is, that most of the houses in the centre of the town being covered with thatch, the place had frequently been visited with desolating fires'. He notes that by 1822 there were 'in the centre of the town scarce any thatched houses'. The river banks were extended in 1794: 'until this time the river below the stone bridge had no proper embankment – there were no roads as at present on its margin, the tide flowing close up to the walls of the houses on both sides'.

The year 1796 was notable:

> The principal streets levelled and paved. Expense £1400, paid by the public funds and statute labour of the Burgh. Before this period the streets were exceedingly rugged and uneven. During the progress of this improvement several old buildings called Forestairs, which projected on the principal streets, were pulled down. At this time also, *Clachnacuddin*, or the *Stone of the Tubs*, which is regarded as the corner stone of the town, was removed from its ancient place in the middle of the High Street, where it had remained from time immemorial, and was set under the Cross, to the great displeasure of many old inhabitants. This stone is mentioned in the notes to the Lord of the Isles, by Sir Walter Scott, who calls it the "Charter Stone of the Burgh".

Sutor records that in 1756 ground was purchased for extending the New Street, now called Academy Street – £250 paid out of Burgh funds.

In 1801 there was a famous incident in the town centre in which a quantity of gunpowder exploded, killing seven people and injuring many others. The fabric of the town was also affected – Sutor notes that 'almost all the houses in the middle of the town were injured, and had their windows shattered on this occasion'. The New or Wooden Bridge was built in 1808, at a cost of £4,000 paid partly by public and private subscriptions, with the balance paid by the feuars of Merkinch – 'soon after the building of this bridge spacious approaches to it were formed on both sides of the river'. Then, in

1809, 'an embankment and footway was formed between the new bridge and Douglas Row'. Thornbush Pier was built in 1815, at a cost of £3,300, 'raised by the Town Council on loan, to be paid by new shore dues. It was able to accommodate vessels of 300 tons.

The New Bridge was repaired further in 1817, with an extra £852 paid by the Burgh; Bridge Street was widened and improved at public expense and a fund of £513 was raised by subscription, 'to relieve the labouring poor who were employed in extending the banks of the river, and forming bleaching greens along its sides.' Sutor gives the population of Inverness town and parish as:

1791	7930
1801	8732
1811	10757
1821	12264

Sutor closes his little book with a discourse on trade and with suggestions for improvements, of which there are many. In some detail he gives us in 1882 what might be seen as the first Structure Plan for Inverness:

1st An Act of Parliament enforcing an adherence to some regular plan, in all new streets and buildings.

2nd New pavement, causeways, and common sewers, for the whole town.

3rd An improved access to the town from the east, by the removal of the collections of manure, stagnant waters, and butchers' slaughter-houses at the Lochgorm; or the extension of the High Street eastwards, by a new line, through the field to the north of Petty Street. The formation of a cross street, from Academy Street to Church Street, opposite the Academy. The extension of Church Street through the Glebe, in a straight line from the Jail spire to the New Bridge. The complete removal of the old buildings called Tolmy Castle, at the lower end of Bridge Street. The completion of the embankments of the river between the bridges. Bridges to the Islands in the Ness, with walks in the Islands, and every practicable improvement and decoration of the promenade on the river banks. A balustrade, new causeway, and projecting footways on the stone bridge. The formation of a new road from the old bridge to Dunain, Dochfour, &c., avoiding Tomnahurich Street. The old bridge being here alluded to, it may be mentioned that the abolition of the trifling tax collected at it from foot passengers, would be very desirable.

4th A spacious Court-house, with accommodations for public functionaries, records, &c.; also a larger Jail and a Bridewell; these are all said to be at present in contemplation. We may add to this, the greater embellishment of the Town Hall, which also ought to contain portraits of the Lord President Forbes, and of the late Provost Inglis – the one the most distinguished, the other the most useful, citizen of Inverness.

5th The lighting of the streets with gas. Leith, a town not much more extensive than Inverness, is about to be lighted with gas.

6th Watchmen, or police officers, to attend on the streets during all hours of the night. The *permanent* employment of some operative road-makers and pavers, to keep the streets and roads in constant repair. An additional number of active scavengers, with more attention to the sweeping of the obscure lanes and alleys of the town. Regulations for the government of porters, common carters &c. And the diminution of the number of small public-houses.

This blueprint for urban improvement has much to commend it. Many of James Sutor's aspirations came to pass, but it certainly rings true today as a wish list which today's citizens would be likely to support.

In his *Reminiscences of a Clachnacuddin Nonagenarian*, published in 1842, John Maclean writes about the old stone bridge, about the Castle, the Old Jail, and Cromwell's Fort. He does say that in his boyhood (in the 1750s and 1760s) 'the town was of very limited dimensions compared with its present state. I remember the time when there were only fifteen smokes and only eight small windows (with the exception of Phopachy House) to be seen between the Blue House (Balnain House) and Ferry'. One passage is worthy of reproduction:

Let me give you a bird's-eye view of the town ninety years ago from the Castle Hill, for which purpose we will ascend by the Castle Wynd . . . From the summit of the old Castle, we obtained, ninety years ago, an excellent view of the town and vicinity; the former then consisted almost entirely of Castle Street, High and Bridge Streets, and Church Street, running at right angles to each other. Then, there was great variety in the height of the different houses, but even those of two and three stories high, were in many instances thatched with straw or heather. At the Shore, nothing in the shape of buildings was to be seen, except the old fort, a few sheds, and the houses of Baile Alves and Mr Pitketlie, which are still standing. The site of the Royal Academy and New Street was a quagmire . . . The land extending east, from the present Academy, along the valley as far as Millburn, was cultivated land in my early days . . . On the hill extending from the Castle, now adorned with villas and hanging gardens that might vie for beauty and luxuriance with those of ancient Babylon, was a spot known as the Gallows Muir, where the extreme punishment of hanging and gibbeting was carried into effect whenever an occasion in the Highlands required, and too frequently on occasions which would now be deemed unworthy of extreme penal affliction.

Maclean has much social detail, of characters and customs from his long life – recording, for example, the appearance of the first umbrella in Inverness: 'It is now 82 years since the natives of Inverness, Nonagenarian among the number, were also astonished at the appearance of an umbrella, which was used in a procession on "St Crispin's day", the 25th of October. Whether it was imported by some daring navigator from China, or from what part of the universe the umbrella came, we can scarcely imagine'.

Writing in 1885, Isobel Anderson, in *Inverness before Railways*, described lyrically the changes in a part of the town she knew well:

No part of the town is more completely changed than the Hill. Drummond, Barnhill, and the Kingsmills and Midmills roads have been completely metamorphosed. The Kingsmills road (if not the very oldest) is one of the oldest in the vicinity of Inverness (the hedges which still border part of it being probably of greater age than any others near the town). And until within a recent period it was one of the most retired. Not many years have elapsed since the only dwelling houses between the entrance of the Midmills road and Milnfield consisted of three thatched cottages, which still exist. Abertarff's old dairy stood where Heathmount is now built, and from it a path called "Goosedubs" branched off between the fields in the direction of what is now called Annfield road, but what was then a very narrow pathway, from which no house could be seen on the lonely old Edinburgh road except the solitary farm-house of

Lilyfield, tenanted by an old man, who went by the name of "Little Angus". Goosedubs was bordered by wild roses and other lovely wild flowers, and formed as secluded and rural a spot for a saunter as could be found near Inverness. Southside Place is now built over the first half of it; and the other half, although still partly bordered by a ragged hedge, is shorn of its former rural beauty, and is a mass of mud and nettles.

Isobel Anderson was writing about a time, thirty-five years before, when 'Old Inverness' was but a memory. There were so many changes in her lifetime that she thought it would be useful to chronicle those she could remember. This passage is typical of the very personal nature of some of her memories:

There have been many changes since those days on the road between the Infirmary and the Suspension Bridge. No Cathedral, no Bishop's Palace, no Collegiate School, no Ardross Terrace had arisen then even in the wildest dreams of the imagination. Beyond Ness House (long levelled to the ground), the residence of Banker John Mackenzie, there stood – where Ardross Terrace stands – the humble houses ranged round "the Little Green". The houses were almost entirely inhabited by washerwomen, who spread out the clothes they washed on the Green, which was not separated from the road by even a paling, and presented a snow-white appearance – it was now closely covered with linen from end to end. Ladies in town often sent their servants with clothes, which had been washed at home, to get them bleached on the Green, and paid one of the washerwomen twopence a night to sit up and watch them. The women took it in turn, to perform this office, and the watcher sat all night at an attic window.

Anderson describes the old Town Hall and the Exchange. In 1885, when *Inverness before Railways* was published, the Town Hall had just been demolished:

In 1847 the old Town Hall, so recently pulled down, was visited by the late Prince Consort in order that he might receive the freedom of the burgh. The Exchange was crowded with spectators, amongst whom the Prince walked slowly, bowing and smiling, so that every one obtained a good view of his features, while his gracious bearing won every heart. The Prince was then on a visit at Dochfour, and he attended one of the Northern Meeting Balls. This visit made 1847 a memorable year for Inverness.

The Exchange in front of the old Town Hall was the place where the hustings were erected at the time of the parliamentary elections. Great riots often took place at those times, and rotten eggs and oranges were freely pelted about, often hitting the candidates as they stood in front of the hustings making speeches to the assembled crowd. At the time when Sir (then Mr.) Alexander Matheson was opposed by Mr. Richard Hartley Kennedy of London, the demonstrations round the hustings were particularly boisterous, and it was quite unsafe to pass along High Street. All the windows opposite the Exchange were crowded with ladies and gentlemen watching the proceedings with keen interest.

As well as vivid memories of buildings still standing, like the 'Blue House' on Huntly Street (now Balnain House), Isobel Anderson has some interesting reflections on the town centre before it was redeveloped:

The Exchange.

Many of the other old dwelling-houses, famed for their hospitality in days gone by, have been turned into offices and shops, as it is now thought unfashionable to live in the town, and every one aspires to a villa in the suburbs.

It was certainly far pleasanter of old to live in the town than it is now; there was little bustle, noise, or confusion in the streets, and as many of the houses were built within courtyards or closes, with only their gables to the streets, and with large gardens behind, with box-bordered walks, and plenty old, shady fruit trees, the occupants could obtain as much quiet and seclusion as if they were living in the country. Several houses of this description on both Church Street and Academy Street, were pulled down to make way for Union Street.

The Station Hotel is built on the site of two handsome and substantial houses, which were approached by flights of steps . . . and were at one time the residences of Provost Grant and Provost Gilzean, although after the former went to reside at the Bught, he used his rooms in town only as offices, to which he drove every morning, from his country mansion.

There were several very neat old-fashioned cottages between Provost Grant's house and the Academy, which were pulled down to make way for the railway station…The opening of the Railway caused truly an immense change in what was once the quietest and most secluded street in Inverness.

Isobel Anderson was very well aware of the tremendous social effects of the coming of the railway:

The habits of the Inverness people have changed much more within the last thirty years than in the sixty years which went before. Since the opening of the Inverness and Nairn railway in 1855, not only have a number of strangers come to reside in the Highland Capital, causing a spirit of competition to arise, and an impetus to be given to progress and activity, but their ever-extending arrival and settlement have caused a gradual but complete revolution in the ways of what had for many years been a quiet exclusive little town, in which the advent of a stranger from the South was an event apt to be regarded with a degree of trepidation as well as excitement. As one new family after another came to settle here, and the heads of the old families died in rapid succession, new manners and customs, the effect of competition and ambition, quickly supplanted the primitive old-fashioned ways which had been handed down from one generation to another.

This endearing mixture of nostalgia with the inevitability of 'progress', with all its benefits, not least to the Anderson family, is typical of her style. She must have been a most interesting woman and no doubt extremely formidable. Her descriptions of the minutiae of daily life and manners show that she regretted the passing of some traditional customs, though one is left with the impression that in some ways she celebrated the liberation from the stringencies of early Victorian social intercourse:

> Of course when the dinner hour was four o'clock, there were no such things in Inverness as hot luncheons and five o'clock teas, but it was the invariable custom to offer wine and cake to every one who called, at whatever hour, or from however short a distance they might come. In fact no visitor to either parlour or kitchen was ever permitted to go away without being asked to eat and drink. A lady coming from only the next street would have considered the hostess to fail strangely in the duties of hospitality if refreshments were not produced. In most houses, a tray with rich cake and sweet biscuits, and with port and sherry (for claret was at that time little used, though it was the favourite beverage of an earlier generation), was laid on a side table in the drawing-room, every forenoon, to be in readiness for any visitors that might happen to call. It was not then thought vulgar to press people to eat, or old-fashioned to introduce guests to one another. It was the rule then, and not the exception, for every gentleman to raise his hat entirely from his head, when bowing to a lady, and to draw off his glove before shaking hands with her. It was also the custom for every gentleman to offer his arm to any lady who might be walking along the street with him.

She also has long descriptions of how Christmas and New Year were celebrated and of how 'Hallowe'en parties were a great institution in Inverness in those days among the upper and middle classes' and of how 'among the lower classes there were many Hallowe'en freaks, which involved going out in disguise along the streets, and, indeed, many young people in the upper classes used to join in these frolics. There was, in fact, no house in Inverness, high or low, where Hallowe'en was not kept'. She also says that 'the first of April, or "gowking day", was "never forgotten by any class" and gives examples of some of the pranks perpetrated on leading citizens.

In his little booklet on the *Old Buildings of Inverness*, published by Inverness Museum and Art Gallery in 1978, William Glashan has a small section on 'Buildings now Demolished'. Of Queen Mary's House, he says:

> It was demolished in 1968 to make way for the Highlands and Islands Development Board block, with Lows and Littlewoods beneath. Mary Queen of Scots stayed there for a short time in 1562 but from that period, only the medieval vaults remained in 1968. Part of them has been rebuilt in the entrance hall of the Highlands and Islands Development Board. The house was ruinous for some time and had been rebuilt and altered several times. The interior was very confused and the staircases led to rooms at various levels in a nightmare fashion. It was a plain building, but the Burgh lost character with its removal.

Queen Mary's House.

Between Queen Mary's House and the Prudential Assurance were two eighteenth-century houses with cornices and balustrades. On the Bank Street side of Queen Mary's House were two pleasant houses with pink stone walls with climbing flowering plants and little gardens and next to them were the Parish Council building and the "Inverness Courier" building. The latter alone remains of the little group, the only bit of Old Inverness for some distance around.

This perhaps serves as a fitting epitaph to this part of the town, by somebody who clearly loved and appreciated the sometimes messy townscape.

Of Castle Tolmie, the medieval building damaged and then demolished in 1849 when the old stone bridge was swept away in a flood, Glashan has an equally sympathetic description:

It had good stone dormer heads which were later built into Redcastle on the Black Isle, but there they have suffered from neglect. A later group of houses called Castle Tolmie was built at the southeast end of the suspension bridge, designed by Robert Carruthers about 1900. These were very good indeed and grouped well with the Castle. Unfortunately they were removed in 1960 to make way for a contemporary block. Before the second Castle Tolmie was built, there was a pleasant row of small houses called Gordon Place, shown in one of Delavault's paintings.

Another notable building in this area to be lost in the 1960s was the Workmen's Club, a classical building with columns and arches. The architect was John Rhind, a former Provost of the Burgh. Glashan also laments the passing of the Northern Meeting Rooms on Church Street, built in 1790 and demolished in 1960. It was, he says, 'a severe classical building with a good and ornate interior, used for great social occasions'. He also describes Lady Drummuir's House, at 43 Church Street. Aged 77 in 1746, she played hostess to both Bonnie Prince Charlie and later to the Duke of Cumberland. This house was demolished in 1843, its demise apparently witnessed with regret by Alexander Ross, father of the architect of the same name.

Also on Church Street was St John's Episcopal Church, designed by Robertson of Elgin, with a fan-vaulted roof and an uncompleted tower. The site became Frasers Auction Rooms and is now a restaurant. At the end of Church Street, beside the Gaelic Church (now a bookshop), stood

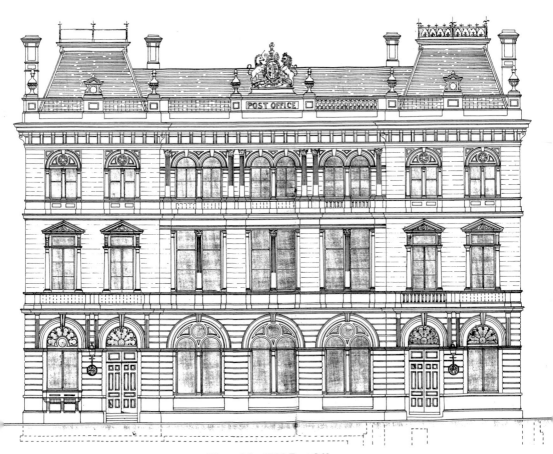

Plan of the 1888 Post Office.

the Technical College, dating from the late eighteenth century. After its demolition the site was left empty and is now a grassy bank.

Glashan has some scathing remarks about the new Post Office on Queensgate:

The present Post Office in Queensgate was built in the 1960s after the demolition of the previous building which was built in 1888. The older office was a very good classical building in Italian Renaissance style, all in sandstone and well detailed. While it was probably necessary to enlarge the building, it is not clear why the front could not have been retained or rebuilt. The new front is of the same width and height as before and has the same number of windows and doors, but the original local sandstone has been replaced by drab grey concrete facings and a dog-toothed "cornice".

Glashan also mentions the Methodist Church in Union Street, originally the Music Hall, with shops beneath. It was destroyed by fire in 1961. Perhaps surprisingly, he laments the loss of the Gas Holder on George Street. It was, he says:

> . . . the most dominating feature in the town when seen from a distance. It was well-proportioned and as it was encased it did not change its height like its successor at Seafield – it remained clean and tidy. It was demolished in 1978, and although not liked, I think it was a loss.

All too sadly typical of the fate of old buildings are two examples with which William Glashan closes his brief summary of recent losses:

> Mile End Cottage, which stood on a side road near the canal bridge leading from the Fort William Road to Craig Dunain, was the last thatched cottage in Inverness. It was vacated in the late 1950s and rapidly fell into decay. Everything that could be moved was stolen and the stones were removed, presumably by boys, and dropped into a nearby lochan. The cottage made a pretty picture with its background of hills and a line of trees in front (since cut down). Two old ladies lived there with an old black dog. There was a little windmill in front and a pump behind.
>
> The surroundings of the King's Mills on the road to Culcabock were greatly altered by road alterations in 1978. The water-wheel is gone – a good overshot wheel. There was an old cottage with cart sheds attached just opposite the mill. An old man lived in the cottage and there were two brown and white cats who came out of the mill to be stroked. Another pretty picture gone.

William Glashan was born in Aberdeen in 1903, an architect by profession, who had lived and worked in Inverness for 30 years when *Old Buildings of Inverness* was published in 1978. He was involved in many restoration projects, most notably at Bow Court, Inverness, in 1970. These are the buildings adjoining Dunbar's Hospital on Church Street. His designs were used at St Maelrubha's Church, Poolewe, and in extensions to the Baptist Church in Inverness. He was Depute Architect to the Northern Regional Hospital Board from 1949 to 1970. He quotes an appropriate passage from 1 *Corinthians*, chapter 15, verse 6:

'. . . of whom the greater part remain unto this present but some are fallen asleep.'

There is perhaps no better way of describing the lost buildings of Inverness.

Edward Meldrum was an Aberdonian and an architect, who painstakingly recorded the local history of Inverness and surrounding areas in a series of pamphlets published in the 1980s. He was a President of the Inverness Field Club and a Chairman of the Georgian Society's Highland Group, dedicated to the study and protection of Scots architecture. Professionally he was involved in architectural restoration work in the Highlands. His historical research was thorough and his local knowledge was unrivalled; his work was published in rather dense text and would certainly repay re-publication today in a more accessible format. *Inverness: Local History*

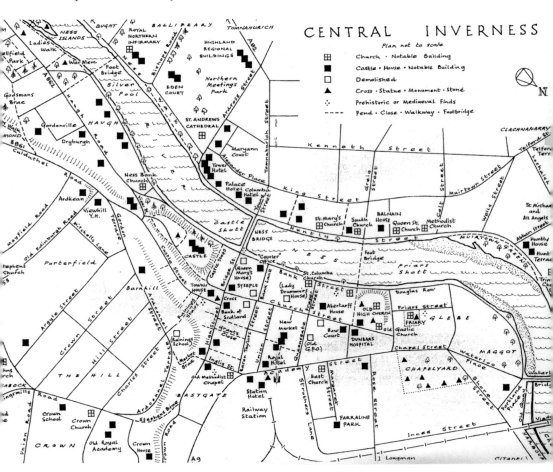

Meldrum's map of central Inverness.

and Archaeology Guidebook No 4, published in 1982, covers the townscape of Inverness.

Meldrum was very aware of the importance of the coming of the railways to Inverness. The Lochgorm Railway Workshops designed and built locomotives for the Highland Railway from 1869. Next door to the station an area of wholesale warehouses and industrial premises grew up in Falcon Square (named after the Falcon Foundry) and Dempster Gardens – all now swept away for the second phase of the Eastgate development, except for what was regarded as the only structure of architectural merit, which was demolished and rebuilt as one side of the new Falcon Square. Traders who occupied these buildings would, in older times, have traded from stores and workshops at the harbour.

Perhaps showing professional solidarity, Meldrum is relatively kind when referring to some of the more disappointing architectural developments of recent decades:

By the outbreak of the First World War in 1914, Inverness had been enhanced by more good buildings, including several churches and church halls, and the completion of Union Street and Queensgate by Walter Carruthers and Alistair Ross, son of Dr. Ross. The severe economic depression between the two World Wars seriously affected local industries and the building trade in particular . . . Also the trend, much more evident today, of small local businesses being swallowed by larger or even multi-national firms, began in the 1920s...

Financial restrictions have been given as the main apology for the poor quality and design of buildings erected between the two World Wars and after, in Inverness and other Scots towns; but the lowered status of the profession of architecture could also be a contributory factor. Certainly many buildings went up – mostly private enterprise and public authority housing. In the 1930s the former was often called "jerry-building", the latter was officially built to certain "standards", the criterion being low cost. The axiom "buy cheap, buy dear" is never so true as when applied to building, as present-day soaring maintenance costs of "council houses" are proving.

The relative affluence of the 1960s brought changes in shopping trends: many commercial businesses closed, or moved out of the town centre, their premises being taken over by offices, such as building societies and credit and finance companies, with frontages similar to shops, or by impersonal supermarket stores . . . These new shopping markets, and office blocks and multi-storey car parks, usually of an uninteresting design and poor appearance mark the beginning of the end of the so-called "Modern movement" in architecture. Fortunately Inverness has not too many examples of such, and has escaped the sad effects of the high multi-storey flatted housing, prevalent in southern cities and towns.

Therefore, despite the fact that it cannot be considered a true Highland capital city, and although the heart of what was essentially a Victorian "railway-age" town has been very ruthlessly torn apart by ugly development blocks – many produced by central government agencies – Inverness still retains something of its old pleasing skyline fronting the lovely River Ness, with its tree-clad banks and picturesque islands. These scenic amenities, together with some elegant old buildings and a few gracious mansions, remain to encourage those who wish and hope to see, by preservation and conservation, a future enlightened interest awaking in both Invernessians and incomers, so that our surviving heritage of historic and handsome buildings can be blended sympathetically and aesthetically into any new planned environment. Only in this way can future developments be absorbed into and assimilated with the uncertain present and the ancient past of the Royal and Ancient Burgh of Inverness.

So, it could have been worse – much worse.

Meldrum's little pamphlet is perhaps our main source for a brief account of the lost buildings of Bridge Street, and so is worthy quoting at some length:

The south side of Bridge Street (Brig Gait or Bridgend) was part of the Royal Castlehill and for defensive reasons was possibly not built up until later medieval times. The present shopping/office development here occupies the sites of several interesting and historic buildings, all swept away in the demolitions and street-widening of 1959-62. On the west side of Castle Wynd, which, unlike Castle Street, had been the main access from the City Centre to the Castle, stood the Burgh Police Court and Offices, under which an arched pend led down the Castle Steps to the riverside, and adjacent was the original Burgh Library and Museum, designed by Alexander

Ross, Architect, and opened in 1883 by Charles Fraser-Mackintosh MP. On this site now stands the Inverness Museum, ugly externally, but well worth a visit . . .

Fronting on to Bridge Street, before demolition, were several buildings, mostly late eighteenth or early nineteenth-century in date, with pends leading to old closes and courts, where some houses retained characteristics of the sixteenth and seventeenth centuries. A mutilated, but once fine roll-moulded marriage lintel and fireplace surround was uncovered in 1962 behind No 5 against the old Library's west wall . . . Behind Nos 11 and 13 was the Albion Hotel with a once-picturesque courtyard and three flights of forestairs: the corbiestep-gabled buildings backing on to Castle Steps had a skewputt dated 1756 and the initials K McK and E S.

Behind No 17 the basement of the house at the head of the close was barrel-vaulted, probably of sixteenth-century date, and in the south-east corner was a rectangular aumbry recess, and a door opening leading to a turnpike stairway, later blocked up, to upper floors. The Workmen's Club (Nos 19-23), built 1871, had a good classical façade with double columns between arcaded windows at first floor level – John Rhind, Architect.

Watt's Hotel Close (between Nos 23 and 25) led to one of the town's few temperance hotels, and under the higher open area next to Castle Steps was uncovered, during building work, the fragmentary remains of stone walling, with the base of a small round tower possibly part of the medieval defensive outworks at the north-west base of the Castle Hill. At the south-west end of Bridge Street stood, till the end of the eighteenth century, the town lodging of the Robertsons of Inshes: the building not only projected into the narrow thoroughfare, but allowed a very restricted access through an alley to the riverside under the Castle Hill. In this lodging until the early eighteenth century, the Burgh Council met in the "Laigh Council House", and on this site, facing the river, there later stood three two-storey houses known as Gordon Place, which was the name of what is now Castle Road, laid out when the stone retaining wall of the Castle Hill was built about 1800 – previously only a path ran along the bank. In these houses, when demolished in 1900, were discovered inscribed stones with initials and a lintel dated 1604, perhaps built in from the older Inshes lodging: the site was then occupied by a block of buildings, known as the new "Castle Tolmie"

(William Carruthers, Architect) to be removed in 1959 preparatory to the replacement of the Suspension Bridge.

From these notes, it is clear that the demolition of these buildings was not only an unrivalled example of cultural vandalism, but also a missed opportunity to learn more archaeologically about the history of Inverness over several centuries. Continuing Meldrum's tale of woe, and omitting his descriptions of successive bridges over the Ness at the foot of Bridge Street, he takes up the story on the other side of the road:

At the west end of Bridge Street's north side stood, until its regrettable demolition – agreed to by the Secretary of State – in 1968, one of the most historic buildings of Inverness – Queen Mary's House, so called because of its occupation by that monarch in 1562 while her army laid siege to the Castle. Although much altered at first and second floors by William Inglis of Kingsmills in 1787, when the external forestairs and pedimented dormers were removed, with the two internal turnpike stairs, there remained of the original sixteenth-century house, the barrel-vaulted ground floor, with its 1½ m (5ft) thick walls, the round moulded arched pend (later filled by window) leading to a cobbled back court, and most of the external walls to eaves level. The external frontage was altered by blocking some of the medieval small windows and regularising the fenestrations in the classical manner; internally the altered apartments had very good eighteenth-century work in the moulded ceilings, wooden panelling, fireplace surrounds, shuttered small-paned windows, and mural cupboards. From the late eighteenth century till demolition it had been the premises of wine and spirit merchants, including Fraser, Wilson & Co., later John Ferguson (Provost 1836–9) and latterly, after 1890, Mackintosh, Macleod & Co.

Between this old house and the river stood, until it was undermined by the 1849 spate and demolished in 1852, the seventeenth-century town lodging of the Forbeses of Culloden, later called "Castle Tolmie" because the owner, in 1796, was William Tolmie. This old picturesque building – with its corbiestep gables, corner turrets and turnpike stairs – protruded into Bridge Street with only a narrow wynd giving access to what later became Bank Street; originally it may have been a town lodging of the Frasers, as dormer pediments bore Fraser coats-of-arms, with initials JS and HF and date 1678;

a fireplace marriage lintel in the main room had the same date and initials, with the text, "Christ is my Life and Rent. His Promise is my Evident". By the 1840s the building had deteriorated to the status of a third-class hostelry, and, following its demolition, three of the sculptured dormer pediments were subsequently rebuilt during restoration at Redcastle, on the Black Isle.

In these prosaic accounts of now missing buildings it is possible to detect the pain and resentment disguised by Meldrum's architectural professionalism. Throughout his little pamphlet are numerous references to demolished buildings. For example:

At the corner of High Street and Castle Street stood, till demolition in 1955, the old YMCA and MacKay's Clan Tartan Warehouse building, dating from 1868 – Architect, John Rhind. Its high Corinthian columns and heavy balustrading made this the burgh's most flamboyant corner edifice, its bold classicism complementing the Bank of Scotland opposite. Surmounting the corner columns above the entrance was a group of three statues representing the Graces, known locally as "Faith, Hope and Charity".

Meldrum's descriptions of surviving buildings are equally well informed, with revealing detail. Amongst his notes on the buildings of Church Street is this account of the Northern Meeting Rooms, in its day one of the most important venues in Inverness for public events:

Turn into Church Street, where the south corner of Baron Taylor's Street was occupied by the Northern Meeting Rooms, a large plain structure built 1790 and demolished in 1963; its main symmetrical frontage to Church Street had originally a columned portico projecting over the pavement. After the founding of the Northern Meeting in 1788, assemblies, balls, banquets and other important social functions were held here. Opposite at the corner of Bank Lane – originally the west extension of the Back Vennel – stood until demolition in 1968, No 23 Church Street, the symmetrical Renaissance-style eighteenth-century town house probably built by John Mackintosh of Aberarder, who, between 1794 and 1803, was Provost for two terms of office; about 1830 it became the Inverness branch of the National Bank.

Down towards the river, beside the building which in Meldrum's day was still the 'Courier Office', was 'the nineteenth-century Parish Council Office building (demolished 1968), with a columned and balustraded entrance porch and ogee-gabled dormer windows'.

Although most of the demolitions took place in the town centre, there were occasional depredations elsewhere. At the top of Raining's Stairs, says Meldrum:

> Raining's School, regrettably demolished for no good reason in 1976, was a plain, sturdy Georgian building of three storeys, built in 1757, possibly from a design by John Adam, Architect, one of the famous Adam brothers. It was started as a school by the Society for the Propagation of Christian Knowledge following a bequest in 1727 from John Raining of Norwich; extensions were built between

Inverness Castle from Raining's Stairs.

1840 and 1881 – by 1894 the pupils had been transferred to the nearby High School.

Close by, at the top of Stephen's Brae, the lands of the old barony of Auldcastlehill were bought in 1806 by Col. Archibald Fraser of Lovat, who built Crown House in 1815. This was an important residence, but sadly only part of it survives:

This House, on Crown Avenue, consisted of the original central mansion, sometimes called Abertarff, with later wings, that on the east having a fine columned doorway, while on the north side are two semi-circular projections with dormers. The west wing of the House was demolished, despite protests, in 1978 and replaced by an unsightly building completely out of character with the other Victorian and Edwardian properties on Crown Avenue.

Edward Meldrum, when President of the Inverness Field Club, wrote in an introductory essay to *Old Inverness in Pictures* (1978):

Good building and sensitive planning in Inverness ended after the first decade of the twentieth century. Following the First World War there was a lowering of standards. The change came with the adoption of cheap and nasty 'jerry-building', and both public authority and private developments reflected lack of architectural character and loss of sense of good-mannered townscape, due partly to shortage of finance but largely to paucity of imaginative design. The Invernessian-in-the-street's impression, rightly or wrongly, is that architecture and planning have, since the Second World War, combined to produce buildings of outstanding ugliness and lack of elegance in their exterior aspects, although, paradoxically, present-day interior design and planning is generally far more imaginative than that of last century's architects.

The pattern emerging from all this is that, by the mid-nineteenth century, the town centre of Inverness was a mixture of outstanding public and commercial buildings, with town houses for many of the leading families of this part of the Highlands. Almost all of these town houses are gone: Lady Drummuir's House has already been mentioned; Dalcross's House, demolished in 1900, stood at the corner of Queensgate and Church Street.

Only Abertarff House on Church Street survives, typical of its class, and a reminder of what we have lost. Edward Meldrum's booklet contains a very useful map of the town centre (see page 41) on which many of the buildings he describes are marked, together with a key indicating those now demolished. Amongst the notable buildings were structures dating in parts back to the Middle Ages, all tidied up with mid Victorian enthusiasm as the layout of the town centre was 'modernised'. It is undoubtedly the case that our Victorian ancestors were responsible for more demolition of our architectural heritage than anybody else, though in the 1960s and 1980s we tried hard to catch up. We would like to think that today we know better and value our cultural heritage more, but although there are some grounds for optimism there is certainly no room for complacency.

Elizabeth Grant of Rothiemurchus (1797–1885) has an interesting account of the Northern Meeting Rooms on Church Street in 1814.

The Northern Meeting was to all of our degree as important a gathering as was the Badenoch Tryst to our humbler acquaintance. It had been set going soon after my birth by her who was the life of all circles she entered, the Duchess of Gordon. She had persuaded all the northern counties to come together once a year about the middle of October, and spend the better part of a week at Inverness. There were dinners and balls in the evenings; the mornings were devoted to visiting neighbouring friends and the beautiful scenery abounding on all sides . . . The annual meeting went on [after the death of its founder], bringing many together who otherwise might not have become acquainted, renewing old intimacies, and sometimes obliterating old grudges.

We put up at Mr. Cooper's good house in Church Street, where we were made very welcome and very comfortable; and being tired with our day's work, we enjoyed a quiet evening with Mrs. Cooper and her girls. We had come purposely the day before the first ball for the rest. The next morning I was sent with some of the children to Castle Hill, a very pretty farm of Mr. Cooper's three miles from Inverness. We came back in time for me to get my toilette laid out ready, and my mother's too, with help, and to have my hair dressed by Mr. Urquhart.

Probably all young girls have felt once in their lives, at least, as I felt on mounting the broad, handsome staircase of the Northern Meeting rooms on my father's arm. The hall was well lit, the music sounded joyously, and my heart beat so high, it might have been seen to palpitate! My mother and I passed into a suite of waiting-rooms, where poor Peggy Davidson's aunt attended to take care of the wraps, then rejoining my father we entered, through the large folding-doors, our fine assembly rooms. All was noise and blaze and mob. I could neither see nor hear distinctly… We were really acquainted with almost everybody, and of kin to a great number.

In *Inverness: A History and Celebration of the City* (2005), Jamie Gaukroger and Clare Maclean provide well-researched text to accompany Francis Frith Collection photographs of Inverness. Their comments on the 1960s Bridge Street developments are well made:

The meetings for this redevelopment took place in private and without much input from the general population. The old shops and buildings were torn down, and in their place came the concrete blocks that are still a feature of the town today. Sad to say, they are somewhat uninspiring as buildings. There were even mutterings about applying for Millennium funding to tear them down. In fact, the rebuilding of the 1960s lacked any of the flair of the rebuilding of Inverness during the Victorian age. The old post office was demolished and replaced with the block that stands on the Queensgate today; the Victorian façade of the railway station was replaced; and the Caledonian Hotel, once so famous, was rebuilt as another concrete block – not, perhaps, Inverness's finest hour architecturally speaking.

Written in 1995, John Macmillan Pearson's little guide book, *A Guided Walk around Inverness*, gives interesting sketch maps and drawings of many Inverness buildings and streetscapes. Published by the Inverness Civic Trust, Pearson's book attempts a more even-handed assessment:

Bridge Street was formerly known as Brig Gait – brig being Scots for bridge and gait meaning street or way. Bridge Street leads down to the River Ness where there has been a bridge on this site since the reign of King Alexander in 1214–1249. Continue on under the canopy of Castle Wynd to the pedestrian crossing. This modern development overhead was set back from the old street line and consequently has opened up this end of the street. As we will see on our walk the proportion of street width to building height plays an important part in our experience of the town. The modern development of Bridge Street houses the offices of the Highlands and Islands Development Board above Littlewoods store. While waiting for the 'green man' this is an ideal opportunity to compare the straightforward appearance of the modern development with the adjacent nineteenth century buildings. Besides the contrast in scale between old and new the eye immediately takes in the repetitive modern façade, yet is absorbed by the intricacy and detail of the older Georgian buildings. The latter arouses interest and contributes more towards the quality of the street scene.

There have been several published collections of old photographs of Inverness. Inverness Field Club produced *Old Inverness in Pictures* in 1978, under the editorship of Loraine MacLean of Dochgarroch. The *Inverness Courier* published *Joseph Cook's Inverness* in 1992. Both collections have authoritative text and captions to accompany the photographs. Jamie Gaukroger and Clare Maclean attempted a more comprehensive overview in *Inverness: A History and Celebration* (2005), their book of photographs of Inverness from the Francis Frith Collection, though sadly their publisher, the bookshop Ottakar's, went out of business soon after their book was published and it did not get the circulation or recognition it deserved.

The Inverness Local History Forum, through its *Inverness Remembered* books, has made an important contribution to Inverness history by collecting and recording memories of the twentieth century, by interviewing elderly residents in care homes – and in some cases each other. Their books are full of social and historical detail and bring the authentic voice of the people to the next generation. The books are lavishly illustrated with photographs, often provided by the participants.

Two books by the current author are of interest. In 1996 the Edinburgh publisher John Donald produced *The Life and Times of Inverness*, which invites Invernessians to consider more closely available sources for the study of local history; in 2006 Breedon Books published *Inverness: Highland Town to Millennium City*, with many historic photographs and illustrations.

Most recently, in 2004 Birlinn published *Inverness*, by James Miller, which is a comprehensive history of the town, bringing the story of the Highland capital into the twenty-first century. Scattered through its pages are a surprising number of accounts of buildings in Inverness being destroyed by fire, throughout its long history. This book is well researched and addresses the horrors of the 1960s in some detail.

Built by Joseph Mitchell in 1835, the property of Viewhill was gutted by fire and is threatened with demolition after local councillors approved this course of action at the end of 2009. In recent times it served as a youth hostel. Edward Meldrum gives a succinct description:

At the corner of Gordon Terrace is Viewhill, built in 1835 as his residence by Joseph Mitchell, Civil and Railway Engineer (1803–1883); the house was designed in the Romantic tradition, with an inscribed quotation from Shakespeare's *Macbeth* (Duncan's opening lines, Act 1, Scene 6) on a bronze plaque over the entrance door; over the side entrance gate is the Latin tag (now partly worn away) "Sapiens qui assiduus" – "Wise is he who is diligent". A fine wide Gothic-style archway – Viewhill Gate – leads to Mitchell's Lane, the only thoroughfare named after the town's most famous engineer of the Victorian era.

For those of a curious disposition, the Shakespearean lines, uttered by Duncan at Macbeth's castle in Inverness, are:

This castle hath a pleasant seat; the air
Nimbly and sweetly recommends itself
Unto our gentle senses.

In the summer of 2012 there seemed to be some cause for cautious optimism, as independent consultants appeared to suggest that it would be better if this important building was preserved, an assessment confirmed by Historic Scotland.

In the Bught area of Inverness, Bught House, a two-storeyed eighteenth-century Georgian house, was demolished in 1967 to make way for an ice-rink. The house had a projecting entrance wing and Victorian-style eaves battlementing added in the nineteenth century. The estate was bought by Inverness Town Council in 1923, proving that public ownership is no defence against 'progress'.

Falcon Square takes its name from Falcon Foundry, which closed before 1900. In the 1860s the lands known as Dempster's Parks were laid out in a 'gridiron' layout to cater for light industrial workshops and warehouses. Meldrum gives a useful summary:

Before railways the area from Hamilton Street eastwards to Loch Gorm was known as Dempster's Parks and here quarrels were settled by duelling before this murderous practice ceased about the 1840s. After the 1860s the parks became built up, to a "gridiron" layout plan, as the town's first industrial area, catering for whole-sale commerce and business from the railhead's goods traffic. The narrow causewayed and cobbled streets with their warehouses and stores were numbered First Street (or Washington Court, after the Washington Hotel on Hamilton Street) and Second, Third and Fourth Streets, the last three however being still colloquially known as Dempster's Gardens: Fourth Street was called Tobacco Street in the 1860s. All these streets were cleared during the 1970s pre-paratory to the construction of the present Eastgate commercial development scheme.

This area, with its cobbled streets and rectilinear gird, adjoining the railway station and marshalling yards, was the town's first industrial zone. Today we would call it an industrial estate.

Another useful book on the history of Inverness is *Historic Inverness* (1981), by A. Gerald Pollitt. Gerald Pollitt was a Lancastrian who settled in Inverness with his Scottish wife and served on the Town Council from 1954 until local government reorganisation in 1975. His book, though full of historical detail, is surprisingly short of architectural information, especially on demolished buildings. He seems not to disapprove of the modernisation of Bridge Street, and indeed the picture on the cover of his book, captioned 'Inverness: ancient and modern', displays the boxlike buildings of the HIDB headquarters and the Caledonian Hotel with perhaps just a hint of irony as dark storm clouds gather over the town and a rainbow ends at the 'graceful lines' of the new bridge.

CHAPTER 5

INVERNESS REMEMBERED

In an 'unashamedly nostalgic' collection of memories published in 2004 by the Inverness Local History Forum, there is much detail of life in Inverness in the twentieth century. Many of the places described are gone, but many still remain, although the way of life described is gone forever. The collection, compiled and edited by Sheila S. Mackay OBE, appeared under the title *Inverness, Our Story: "Mind Thon time"*. It is based on recorded interviews from over 80 informants. This passage (pp. 85–6) gives a flavour:

> Victoria Square was where the Rose Street multi-storey car park is now. My granny lived at No 8 and we were at No 9 and my other grandparents lived at No 50 Rose Street. All the family, aunts and uncles stayed round about. I went to the Bell School for about a year or so and then we all went up to the Crown School because the Territorials were taking over Farraline Park (1936/37). Farraline Park was a big enclosed square with the Bell School at the top, then the back entrance to the Rose Street hall on the left and the Lodge where Charlie's Café is now. There were big metal gates into the park and a lot of the TA were based there. On the way to school I would come out of Victoria Square on to Strothers Lane and cross over through the back station at Platform 7 past the old railway laundry, then through Falcon Square and we'd come out on Eastgate where the Northern Ignition and the blacksmiths were. On the way home from school we came down Stephen's Brae and down the little steps at the bottom of Crown Road and crossed over to stand at the blacksmith's watching the horses.
>
> I remember on Rose Street there was the Foundry and on the left was the Gas Works. Mrs Aitken's shop was on the corner of Rose Street and Innes Street, there were little shops on all the corners then. Our little shop was on the corner of Rose Street and Milne's Buildings, that was Duncan Urquhart's and Betty Macrae was the assistant there for years. On the other corner there was a little

wooden shed we called 'Bronyan's'. This was a Mr MacDonald and he used to sit on an upturned wooden box. His family stayed in a flat at the top of Rose Street but old 'Bronyan' he would sit on top of his box and fall asleep and there was all those little cardboard boxes in front of him full of sweeties and he also sold paraffin. There used to be an overwhelming smell of paraffin in the shop. If anybody was to drop a match the whole place would have exploded. In 1948 we moved to Dalneigh and not long after the Victoria Square came down.

Later in the same volume (p. 328) Victoria Square features again:

Many a time I stood in Victoria Square and watched the railwaymen come from their work, hundreds of them, the place was black with them. There were hundreds worked on the railway then (1920s). My father worked on the railway, on the engines. It was quite a good job then, them and the Rose Street Foundry, these were the two main works.

A second volume of reminiscences was published in 2007, with the recollections of another 71 informants. This extract from the Foreword by Sheila Mackay gives some idea of the motivations of the Inverness Remembered project:

Our tales start before the war, WWI when many families lived in housing conditions which simply wouldn't be tolerated today. Many have related accounts of the older parts of the town from the Shore to Merkinch, Castle Street to the Haugh, where the sanitary arrangements were primitive to say the least. And yet, despite the poor housing and living standards, whole communities and generations of local families lived and worked side by side and usually helping each other when times got tough. Yes, of course, there was the odd falling out of neighbours, but everyone knew there was nowhere else to go, so they resolved their differences and got on with their lives.

The war years were, for the women everywhere, a testing time, bringing up their families single-handed many of them, and going out to work as well. It was realised as the war years rolled on that when it was eventually over, the men coming home after years away would need and indeed would have more than earned, decent housing to bring up the new families which would be appearing over the next few years. They, and their wives and children deserved better than the conditions they had lived in pre-war. And so the big drive to build decent homes began in the late 40s and where once the farmlands of Hilton and Dalneigh were, the builders moved in and very quickly new homes started to rise from the fields. There was also the new concept of pre-fabs, compact and quickly erected houses, which were appearing at the Carse and various other sites in town.

It may be difficult to picture how the families, especially the mothers who had never had a bathroom or electricity, or indeed indoor toilet facilities, felt when they were allocated a new house in one of the new areas and with all the mod-cons they'd only dreamed about.

It is worth pointing out that 'Inverness Remembered' is the name given by the Inverness Local History Forum to its project to record, transcribe, preserve and publish the memories, reminiscences and recollections of older Invernessians. Subsequently, the *Inverness Courier*, the local newspaper founded in 1817, has published collections of old photographs contributed by its readers, under the title *Inverness Remembered*. So far nine volumes have appeared and more are in prospect.

A book of photographs entitled *Joseph Cook's Inverness* was published by the Inverness Courier in 1992 to commemorate the 175th anniversary of the newspaper. Joseph Cook (1881–1973) was a director of Walker's Sawmills in Inverness. He was a collector of photographs, and assembled a collection of as many different aspects of the history of the town as he could find. It provides a unique record of Inverness from the 1850s to the 1920s.

Over the years various local architects and artists have sketched both existing and lost buildings, usually relying on old photographs, drawings and paintings. Perhaps the most successful was Pierre Delavault, the art master at Inverness Royal Academy, whose pictures of old Inverness were published, in colour, by Robert Carruthers at the Courier Office in Inverness in 1903.

CHAPTER 6

PIERRE DELAVAULT AND OTHER ARTISTS

*

In 1903 the *Inverness Courier* published *Old Inverness*, containing plates from watercolours painted by Pierre Delavault, the French art master at Inverness Academy, with accompanying text. Most of the buildings in his paintings were already history by the time the book appeared, though there were a few survivals, for example Abertarff House and Dunbar's Hospital, both on Church Street. In 1969 the *Courier* republished Delavault's book, with additions, but it is now very rare. There are, of course, copies of both editions in Inverness Library – and digitised images of all plates and text are on Am Baile, The Highland Council's history and culture website (*www.ambaile.org.uk*).

Delavault's plates are often based on earlier drawings and even photographs, and are in colour. They are reprinted in this book as a very welcome and very finely observed supplement to other sources; of course there is a possibility of some artistic licence, but all comparisons with other depictions suggest that he was scrupulous in his research.

Pierre Delavault died at his house, Braehead, on Old Edinburgh Road, on 10 January 1907, aged 48. His obituaries in the Inverness papers remark on his teaching skills, his artistic ability and his personal qualities. He was well known for portraits of private citizens, for his published sketches of old Inverness buildings, and for renovation and repair of pictures belonging to the Town Council. He was a Parisian by birth, who exhibited in the Paris salon. He came to Scotland around 1887 and after a couple of years teaching art at a private school in Aberdeen he was appointed as art master at Inverness Royal Academy, following the death of Mr Smart.

The *Highland News* commented:

> In ordinary life Mr Delavault was quiet, undemonstrative and companionable, and made for himself numerous friends, who will sincerely mourn his death. Mr Delavault married several years ago, and leaves a widow and a little boy, for whom much sympathy is felt in their bereavement.

His wife was Bessie Vincent, originally from Norfolk; she married Pierre Delavault there in 1903 and their son Edward Foley Delavault was born in Inverness a year later. Sadly, a second son, Archibald Pierre Delavault, was born in Ipswich, Suffolk, later in 1907, by which time his mother had moved away from Inverness and Braehead.

Pierre Delavault was a member of the Educational Institute of Scotland, St John's Lodge of Freemasons, and also of the Royal Arch Chapter. In the year before his death he had started providing tuition in French phonetics and phonology. His death was due to heart disease, from which he had suffered for three months. His funeral took place at St Andrew's Cathedral and he is buried in Tomnahurich Cemetery.

The Old Stone Bridge and the Castle

Of this view of the old stone bridge and the Castle, he notes: 'The Castle, standing as in the sketch on our noble Castle Hill, was a much more imposing object than it came to be with the ugly excrescence of a jail attached.' Inverness castle was blown up by the Jacobites in 1746; today's 'castle' was built as a sheriff courthouse in 1834, with the adjoining jail added in 1846, now used for offices and storage by the council and other bodies.

The stone bridge was opened in 1685, replacing a wooden bridge which had collapsed twenty years before. It survived until the morning of 25 January

1849, when it was swept away in a great flood which caused widespread damage and devastation in the north-east of Scotland, especially in the counties of Moray and Nairn. In Inverness a section of the Caledonian Canal collapsed, adding to the rush of water. The last person to cross the old stone bridge was a sailor named Matty Campbell, who according to contemporary reports had to jump over a 'chasm' to save his life.

Also in this illustration is Castle Tolmie – the last house on the north side of Bridge Street. Castle Tolmie was demolished in March 1852 to allow for the approaches to the new Suspension Bridge; its successor on the south side of Bridge Street was demolished in the 1960s to make room for the current bridge.

The old stone bridge was built partly with stone from Cromwell's Fort, down at the harbour, which itself made use of dressed stone from Fortrose Cathedral. Built into the stone bridge was a vault between two of the arches which was used as a prison.

GORDON PLACE

Delavault's view of Gordon Place shows houses which were demolished in 1900 to make way for the replacement Castle Tolmie. In the course of these demolitions a lintel with the date 1604 was discovered, along with other stones from older buildings. The new version of Castle Tolmie was built in a deliberately archaic style, with outside stone stairways and a slated roof using 'old stone slates' taken from a building in Kingussie. In 1800 the slope of the hill came right down to the riverside, with just a narrow footpath for pedestrians.

QUEEN MARY'S HOUSE, 1902

The view of Queen Mary's House, dated 1902, is from the bottom of Bridge Street, looking east. The multi-period construction of what remained is immediately obvious. It took its name from the tradition that Mary, Queen of Scots, lodged there during her visit to Inverness in 1562. By the time Delavault drew the much-altered structures, it was one of very few late medieval buildings surviving in Inverness. His notes are brief: 'The outward appearance of the house, its rather grim Scotchness of outline, and its fine situation, are all better illustrated by the accompanying picture than by any written words.' Who would have thought, in 1900, that the public guardians of the culture and heritage of Inverness could ever muster the corporate municipal stupidity to demolish such a historic building? Certainly not Delavault, who opined: 'Long may it stand, the home of many memories, looking across the hurrying river, and preaching reverence to an irreverent age.'

The Corner of Castle Street

This view of the corner of Castle Street shows the municipal heart of Inverness. To the right is the frontage of the old Town House; in the distance, at the end of High Street, is Eastgate. The shops of the main commercial shopping street are seen to the left of this view, all with their distinctive awnings. It represents the area known as the Exchange at it was around 1867; in April 1868 the buildings on the corner of Castle Street were demolished and the foundation stone laid of the ornate YMCA building, later with a tartan shop on the ground floor. The 1868 building was itself demolished in 1955 and became the premises of the drapery store of Alex. Cameron & Co. Today's modern structure is home to a fast food chain.

THE OLD TOWN HALL

All of the buildings in Pierre Delavault's picture of the old Town Hall are now demolished. The Town Hall itself was built in 1708 and demolished in 1878 to make way for the current structure. This view, showing Castle Street to the left and the Exchange on the right, shows the townscape just before the demolitions. The ground floor of this building housed a public reading room; the middle floor contained the council chamber and council offices; on the top floor were the Dean of Guild's offices.

The building to the right of the Town Hall was originally the town house of Forbes of Culloden. It was in this house that the Duke of Cumberland's officers met after Culloden and according to tradition booted Provost Hossack down the stairs for daring to ask for clemency for injured and captured Jacobites. This house was converted into a hotel known as the Horns, later the Commercial Hotel.

The new Town House, today the most distinguished building in Inverness, was officially opened by the Duke of Edinburgh in April 1882. It is still used for council meetings, though sadly the Town Council of Inverness no longer exists. Somehow the office of Provost survives, along with the chain of office, for the chair of the local area committee of the Highland Council.

The first time the UK cabinet met outside London was on 7 September 1921, in the council chamber. Lloyd George was the Prime Minister and was on holiday in the Highlands – along with most of his Cabinet – when the 'Irish Question' demanded urgent attention. Today it is no longer unusual for the Cabinet to meet outside London.

A Shop on High Street

This view of a shop in High Street shows the property which most Invernessians will associate with the newsagent and stationer John Menzies, now W. H. Smith. It was always a newsagent in the later years of the nineteenth century, though before that it was occupied by a succession of wine merchants. One of these was William Fraser, also known for the quality of tobaccos and snuff which he sold in his shop; now he is perhaps better remembered as the father of Lydia Miller, wife of Hugh Miller of Cromarty, the geologist.

THE OLD POST OFFICE

Delavault's drawing of Inverness Post Office, on the corner of Bank Lane and Church Street, shows the headquarters of postal services in Inverness between 1820 and 1841. The Post Office used several other sites in the town before and after this period, before settling on its current site on Queensgate in 1890. The striking late Victorian purpose-built edifice on Queensgate was demolished in 1966 and replaced by the current anonymous structure.

THE CORNER OF CHURCH STREET AND QUEENSGATE

This view (opposite, top), entitled 'An Old Church Street Corner', shows the corner of Church Street and Queensgate before this house was demolished in the 1850s to make way for the headquarters of the Clydesdale and North of Scotland Bank. Stones carrying the dates 1699 and 1700 were discovered during the demolition and incorporated into the new structure.

ABERTARFF HOUSE

Abertarff House (opposite, bottom) survives, though its surrounds are much altered. The building at No. 71 Church Street was originally described as

Top: Corner of Castle Street and Queensgate.
Bottom: Abertarff House.

'situated in Abertarff's Close' – on land owned by the Frasers of Abertarff. It was not, however, their town house, so the current name is probably technically a mistake. Colonel Archibald Fraser of Lovat, who owned the Abertarff estates in the nineteenth century, built Crown House, overlooking Eastgate, which for a while was also erroneously known as Abertarff House.

It is the sole survival in Inverness of a type of house common in Scottish towns in the late seventeenth and early eighteenth centuries. At one time there were many such houses in Inverness with turnpike stairs, but from the end of the eighteenth century they disappeared rapidly, usually prompted by the need to widen streets and tidy up the urban landscape. For many years it was neglected and in danger of becoming completely dilapidated. It was converted to flats, and came into the ownership of the Commercial Bank, which in 1933 started negotiations with Inverness Town Council to transfer it to public ownership. These discussions dragged on for years, but eventually, in 1963, the National Commercial Bank of Scotland handed it over to the National Trust for Scotland, who for a while used it as office buildings. The NTS decision to 'restore' it by the use of white harling has been criticised for changing the character of the building, so in that sense 'Abertarff House' has been lost.

DUNBAR'S HOSPITAL

Similarly, Dunbar's Hospital survives, also renovated in recent years. Delavault's illustration shows it as it was at the end of the nineteenth century. So, the 'structure' in this illustration which is lost to Inverness is not the building, but the street, with its distinctive cobbling, and the pavement in front of the building, with its large paving slabs.

FRIARS' STREET

This view of Friars' Street, showing thatched cottages, with the Old High Church at the end of the street and a local inhabitant feeding his hens, shows what this part of Inverness was like before all of the buildings on the left side of this picture were demolished to make way for the local telephone exchange. The trees half way down the left hand side mark the location of the cemetery of Greyfriars' Churchyard, around and over which the modern offices were built.

The present parish church dates from 1770 but is almost certainly on the site of earlier churches, of which the tower is probably the only surviving part. In pre-Reformation times the mound on which the church stands was known as St Michael's Hill. The church tower, or at least the lower part of it, is usually thought to be the oldest building in Inverness.

GREYFRIARS' CHURCHYARD

Greyfriars' Churchyard itself, much neglected in this view and not the most salubrious nook today, is largely unchanged, except for occasional vandalism; but of course, as already noted, the surroundings have changed rather a lot. It is probably the oldest churchyard in Inverness. The associated monastery was probably built at the beginning of the thirteenth century, though contemporary charters show that it was associated with the Dominicans or Black Friars. However, the cemetery and the street have used the name Greyfriars since at least 1653, when local records mention that Cromwell's troops used some of the stone from the old monastery for building the fort at the mouth of the Ness.

Few of the stones in this churchyard can be identified, though the warrior in chain-mail is sometimes identified in local tradition with the Earl of Mar who died in 1437, at which date he held the office of Justiciar in Inverness. The other old cemeteries in Inverness are the churchyard of the Old High Church, the Chapel Yard, and of course Tomnahurich Cemetery, opened in 1860 by a private company and subsequently taken over by the town as a municipal cemetery.

THE OLD PILLAR

The Old Pillar, the single stone pillar which survives in the Greyfriars' Churchyard, may be the only surviving trace of the associated monastery, though it may be a much later antiquarian marker. Again, the building in the background, on Friars' Lane, is long gone.

THE ROBERTSONS OF INSHES ENCLOSURE

The Robertsons of Inshes burial enclosure in the Old High Church graveyard survives intact; it was erected in 1663 by Janet Sinclair, the mother of William Robertson of Inshes.

QUEENSGATE

Delavault's view of Queensgate shows just how much the townscape of the centre of Inverness has changed since it was tidied up – or obliterated – by Victorian developers. Local tradition suggests that it takes its name from a bridle path used by Queen Mary on the occasion of her visit to Inverness in 1562. The current street and buildings date from the 1890s. The building in the centre of the background was originally the Inverness branch of the Commercial Bank of Scotland, later the National Commercial Bank. The steeple belongs to the English Free Church, opened in 1852. It soon became known as the Free High. After the union between the Free and United Presbyterian Churches in 1900 it became the United Free High, and after the further union in 1929 between the United Free and Established Churches it ended up as the St Columba High Church of Scotland.

OLD GATEWAY IN CASTLE STREET

The 'Old Gateway in Castle Street' is at what is now No. 51, on the east side of the street. This whole area, including the houses across the road demolished in the 1930s when the collapse of part of the castle mound rendered

71

them uninhabitable, was one of the last parts of the town to retain relics of traditional housing. Over the gateway, though not visible in Delavault's illustration, is a stone with the inscription: 'Feir God, dvt not' (Fear God, doubt not).

Thatched Cottages on the Crown

These thatched cottages (opposite, top) are on land acquired in 1897 by the trustees of the Crown Free Church, who erected a handsome church on the site. Since the 1929 union it has been the Crown Church of Scotland. The tower visible above the cottages originally belonged to the Free Church Institution, founded on Ardconnel Street in 1847 but transferred to the site behind the cottages about forty years later. When the Free Church handed over the property to the local Board of Education it became known as the High School, and when Inverness High School moved across the river in 1937 it took the name with it and this site became the Crown School, now Crown Primary.

These cottages were photographed (opposite, below) before their demolition – the billboards in the picture are for Smith's tobacco, Taylor's songbird seed and the Anchor and Union Castle shipping lines.

THE CLOCK TOWER OF CROMWELL'S FORT

When Delavault rendered 'The Clock Tower of Cromwell's Fort' for his 1903 publication, he did not have the benefit of modern research which seems to show conclusively that the tower almost certainly dates from the 1780s, rather that the 1650s, and is part of the offices of a rope factory. Of some interest, however, is his recording of some humps and bumps which could just

73

be the last surviving traces of the fort, then visible on the ground. The fort was started in 1652 and took five years to complete, though it was in use for the garrison from 1655. It could have accommodated 1,000 men, though it is unlikely that the Inverness garrison was ever that large. Its pentagon, star-shaped plan is well known from contemporary drawings. It was bordered on the west side by the river and elsewhere by a moat, for protection. After the Restoration the stonework of the fort, taken from the old Greyfriars' monastery and from Fortrose Cathedral, and no doubt other ruined buildings in the area, was systematically demolished. It is known that some of the stone was used in building the bridge of 1665. By the 1770s the west side of the Citadel was truncated by the widening of the river, during harbour improvements.

In a report prepared by SUAT Ltd archaeological contractors, entitled *The Clock Tower, Cromwell Road, Inverness: Archaeological Evaluation* (2002), by Bruce Glendinning and David Perry, they reached an unequivocal conclusion: 'All the evidence . . . points towards this tower having nothing to do with Cromwell's Citadel. Rather it appears to have been constructed sometime before 1774, when it was part of the hemp manufactory opened in 1765'.

In May 1652, following the capture of Inverness by Commonwealth forces, work began on the construction of a fort, capable of holding about 2,000 cavalry and infantry. The fort was pentagonal in shape with five bastions and was surrounded by a wet ditch with water channeled from the Ness. Its location meant it could be supplied directly by sea. Two concentric rings of buildings enclosed an open parade ground. The outer ring consisted of stable blocks, each housing 164 horses, with lodgings for 312 men in wooden upper storeys. The inner ring comprised blocks of lodgings, each housing 216 men, making a total garrison of 2,640 men and 820 horses. Office accommodation was provided along the riverside. There was a magazine and granary in the centre of the citadel, a 'great foursquare building' of dressed stone, with a church on the third floor. The surviving clock tower is certainly nothing to do with this building. After the Restoration in 1660 the garrison of 800 men was withdrawn. The fort was occupied for a while by a Scottish garrison under Captain Hamilton; its demolition was ordered in 1662 and it appears that this was carried out by 1688.

THE TOLL-HOUSE

This (opposite, top) is one of the last toll-houses in the area, the only other surviving example being at Clachnaharry. In the distance the town of Inverness is visible, with a smoky haze rising above it. The site is at Stoneyfield,

The Toll-house.

just at the point where the railway and the much widened A96 have reorgan-ised the landscape. These structures recall the days when what little traffic which existed was subject to tolls, collected on every road into the town, levied directly on all traffic to support road maintenance. Writing in 1903, Delavault comments: 'Now the road is very quiet, but the Toll-house remains to remind us of the ways of a past generation.' It must now be one of the least quiet places in the Highlands.

After the 1823 Toll Gate Act, gates and toll-houses were erected, usually on the outskirts of towns and villages. Tolls were collected to finance road maintenance; always unpopular, they were abolished in 1878. Of the Inver-ness toll-houses, only the one at Clachnaharry survives. Drakies Toll-house stood near where the entrance to Raigmore Hospital is now, while the sad ruin of Stoneyfield Toll-house is a tribute to the complete lack of care by the local authority who acquired it in 1969 when the Nairn road was re-aligned. 'How does it come about,' asked Edward Meldrum, 'that acquisition by a public authority, authorised as the caretaker and guardian of our architec-tural heritage, so often becomes a "kiss of death".'

INVERNESS BY PAUL SANDBY

This rather wonderful engraving of Inverness (next page) is by Paul Sandby (1731–1809), the government artist who was stationed in Inverness with the

Early engraving of Inverness by Paul Sandby.

British army and who participated in William Roy's *Military Survey of Scotland*, a map produced between 1747 and 1755. The gentlemen on horseback are army officers, with their red coats. As Inverness Castle was blown up by the Jacobites in 1746 the original must date from before that – or else he has used previous drawings of the Castle and incorporated them into the view he witnessed personally. The barrack block on the right hand side of the Castle was built in 1728 under General Wade, who is remembered in the Highlands still for his road-building. This is perhaps the most detailed surviving view of the old stone bridge, built in 1685 and swept away in 1849.

INVERNESS FROM GODSMAN'S WALK

This view of 'Inverness from Godsman's Walk' (opposite, top) shows the town in 1823. The print says that it was 'drawn on the spot by T. Clark, London, published by Smith & Elder'. Thomas Clark (1820–1876) was a well-known Scottish landscape painter. The prominent building on the left is the Northern Infirmary, opened in 1804 'for the benefit of the whole of the Northern Counties.' The Northern Infirmary was renovated and enlarged in 1927 and 1928, then officially opened by the Duke and Duchess of York on 17 May 1929, after which it was known as the Royal Northern Infirmary. More recently, most of the modern extensions were demolished and it is now the headquarters of UHI, the University of the Highlands and Islands. The old stone bridge, with its seven arches, is accurately depicted.

Inverness from Godsman's Walk by Thomas Clark.

The footpath, which survives in much altered form, takes its name from Captain Godsman, an Englishman who was a factor for the Duke of Gordon, who owned lands in Aultnaskiach. Captain Godsman died in 1808. He landscaped a path across what was then rough moorland, from Culduthel Road to Aultnaskiach cottage, where he lived. After his death there were frequent disputes surrounding public access.

THE SUSPENSION BRIDGE

Little is known about the authorship of this print (previous page), but from internal evidence it is likely to date from around 1856. The Suspension Bridge opened in 1855; the Castle opened in 1834 and the adjoining jail in 1846. The Free High Church, later St Columba's High Church of Scotland, opened in 1852.

INVERNESS MUSEUM

Inverness Museum and Art Gallery (IMAG) is another repository of the history and culture of Inverness. Amongst its treasures are architectural drawings by William Glashan and a painting by J. M. W. Turner. Turner's watercolour is tiny – only six inches by three inches – and typically 'fuzzy', though not lacking in detail. Writing for Hi-Arts, the cultural wing of Highlands and Islands Enterprise, Giles Sutherland wrote about Turner's 1833 work when reviewing an exhibition at IMAG in April 2010:

> Turner's scene shows a hive of human industry with boats navigating the shallow river and passengers embarking and disembarking on the near shore. The town steeple and the old high church steeple can be seen across the river to the south.
>
> Typically, there are no hard lines in Turner's painting and the attention to detail, given its size (approximately 6 inches by 3) is extraordinary. Although great attention has been given to its composition and topographical and architectural accuracy, one is also aware that the real subject is light and shadow, the sense of sky and the play of the muted sunlight on the water.

This painting is displayed only occasionally because, as a watercolour, it would easily fade, but can always be viewed by arrangement when not on display. IMAG has many other paintings and drawings featuring Inverness, and excellent coverage of the prehistory of the town.

CHAPTER 7

THE HIGHLAND RAILWAY

If we think that Inverness has changed a lot in the last fifty years, this is as nothing compared to the changes which took place a century earlier. The catalyst for change in the mid nineteenth century was the coming of the railway.

The Inverness and Nairn Railway was authorised in 1854, and completed, and made operational, in 1855, bringing the Railway Age to the Highland capital. Once under way, the pace of change was rapid, and the railway network developed rapidly. In August 1858 the line from Nairn to Keith was opened, linking up with the Great North of Scotland Railway, and joining Inverness to the growing national rail network. To the north, the railway reached Dingwall in June 1862 and Invergordon in May 1863. Steps were taken to link Inverness more directly to Perth and the south, with the formation of various small companies, all of whom were amalgamated in June 1865 under the name of the Highland Railway. In July 1865 the Dingwall and Skye Railway was formed, itself amalgamated with the Highland Railway in 1880. In July 1871 the Sutherland and Caithness Railway was authorised, and opened in July 1874, with branches to Wick and Thurso; it too amalgamated with the Highland Railway on 31 August 1884.

Once construction was authorised, things proceeded rapidly. For example, when the link to Perth was authorised, to join up to the line which had reached Dunkeld in 1856, the line from Dunkeld to Pitlochry was opened in June 1863, Forres was linked to Aviemore in August 1863, and the complete link was opened in September 1863. The construction of the line linking Aviemore and Carrbridge to Inverness shortened the distance to Perth by twenty-six miles; it was completed in 1898.

From the first Inverness and Nairn Railway in 1855 to the Highland Railway in 1863, with through trains from Inverness to London, took only eight years. It happened so quickly that it took a little longer for Invernessians to realise the full implications. Inverness was now a Railway Town, but without much of the infrastructure. Tourist hotels, guidebooks, tour operators, specialised shops and services – all had to be developed. Inverness

Aerial view of Eastgate, showing the layout of the railway.

had accommodated tourists since the eighteenth century, but never in the numbers now about to descend on the town. Apart from the spin-off of tourism, the Highland Railway in itself became one of the major industries in the town. Hundreds of men – and women – worked for the railway, and dozens of local familes were involved as directors or shareholders and followed its fortunes closely. They were not disappointed, and for some, it made their fortunes.

One name above all is associated with the Highland Railway, that of Joseph Mitchell (1803–1883), an extraordinary civil engineer who also chronicled the changes for which he was largely responsible, in his two volumes of memoirs, *Reminiscences of My Life in the Highlands* (1883–4). He was a little indiscreet about some leading figures in the Highlands, especially in the second volume of his memoirs, published 'privately' after his death. Both volumes were fortunately reprinted in 1971, with the welcome addition of an index. His *Reminiscences* are an excellent source for information about the people who brought the Railway Age to the Highlands.

Joseph Mitchell spent his boyhood in Inverness. His father was a super-intendent of public works, in charge of overseeing the many improvements in roads, bridges and harbours throughout the Highlands, working closely with Thomas Telford, whose main task was to complete the Caledonian Canal. He was eventually appointed General Inspector of Roads and moved to Inverness, where the Mitchell family lived in a canal house on the west side of the river. Joseph Mitchell's description of Inverness, around the year 1810, is worthy of inclusion here:

> The town on the west side of the river consisted then mainly of wretched little cottages or huts, occupied by peasantry and working people, many of them employed at the works of the Caledonian Canal. War was then raging in the Peninsula. A party of recruiting soldiers used to parade the street twice a week, with band and pipers, preceded by a dozen or twenty sergeants, gaily decorated with ribbons, and walking with drawn swords. There was therefore a great military taste throughout the population. The men who had returned from the wars, and who were engaged in recruiting, resided with their parents or friends in the cottages at Muirtown, and I used to make friends with them. I admired their beautiful dress, and had the privilege of putting on their belts and bonnets, and listened to their foreign adventures with great interest and delight.

Joseph Mitchell attended the Royal Academy, established in 1791, and obviously enjoyed his time there, in the company of the young sons of all the landed proprietors of the county:

> At that time, besides the territorial chiefs, there were numerous small proprietors throughout the North, many of them related to the great houses. Selling a property except to a native was unknown; indeed, nobody would buy, for the North was separated by distance and difficulty of communication from the outer world. The small proprietors brought up their families with the feelings, tastes, and habits of gentle-folks, and when educated, the young men went forth into the world, and many became distinguished men.
>
> The Inverness Academy was a training-school for many years for these young men. Still, though much had been done for the town, it was nevertheless a poor place. In 1810, it consisted of Bridge Street, High Street, and Church Street, with a beautiful and

venerable old bridge, built in 1685 by subscription, and afterwards swept away by the great flood of 1849. The houses were almost all old, apparently built before 1745. Some of them were of considerable size, with turnpikes and pepper boxes outside, and narrow closes branching off. They were adorned with coats of arms and mottoes.

All beyond were rows of wretched huts. Petty Street, Maggot, and the west side of the river, consisted of a congregation of huts of the worst class, inhabited by the common people. Among them were a few good houses, but the outskirts of the town consisted chiefly of such wretched thatched hovels as I have described.

Joseph Mitchell went on to enjoy a distinguished career as the principal engineer with the Highland Railway Company. He served on the Town Council and was a Director of the Caledonian Bank. He died in London in November 1883, but his body was brought back to Inverness, to his villa at Viewhill, and he was buried in Tomnahurich Cemetery. He left £130,000 in his will; he gave generous donations to the Inverness Soup Kitchen and to the Inverness Coal Fund, and in 1873 he had given £500 towards the foundation of a Free Library in Inverness – it was opened on 16 June 1883. The first printed catalogue of Inverness Public Library, compiled by the Librarian, John Whyte, in 1883, is dedicated to Joseph Mitchell, Esq., of Viewhill, Inverness, 'whose munificent liberality has mainly contributed to the institution and equipment of the Library'.

It is ironic, in the context of this book, that Joseph Mitchell's villa at Viewhill, on Old Edinburgh Road, is threatened with demolition following a disastrous fire. Negotiations continue. His Railway Bridge at Inverness, opened on 11 June 1862, fell down in 1989 following torrential rain and floods and was replaced in 1990.

The Railway Age brought a new range of possibilities for ways in which the working classes of Victorian Inverness could occupy their time. Railway excursions were a feature of the summer months, often arranged by the railway companies in conjunction with annual events such as agricultural shows, or on public holidays when special trains were run, for example, to the beach at Nairn.

One of the pivotal figures in the mid-Victorian redevelopment of the town centre was Charles Fraser-Mackintosh (1828–1901), lawyer, MP, writer and antiquarian. Born on 5 June 1828 at Dochnalurg, Dochgarroch, near Inverness, this influential but modest man was the son of Alexander Fraser, tacksman of Dochnalurg, who belonged to a branch of the large and extensive

Fraser clan descended from William Fraser, second son of Thomas, the fourth Lord Fraser of Lovat, who was killed at the battle of Blar-nan-leine in 1554. This was the famous 'battle of the shirts'.

Two of the three sons of his father's grandfather, Alexander Fraser, who lived at Achnabodach (now Charlestown) on the estate of Kinmylies (from which Charlestown Academy takes its name), joined the Jacobite Rising of 1715, were taken prisoner, and transported to the American plantations. Eventually they settled in South Carolina, where several of their descendants occupied prominent positions as merchants in another Charlestown.

Charles Fraser's mother was Marjory, daughter of Alexander Mackintosh, tacksman of Dochgarroch, whose father William was the eldest son of Duncan Mackintosh, a younger brother of the famous Brigadier Mackintosh of Borlum who was a Captain in Mackintosh's Regiment in the 1715 Rising.

Thus, from both sides of his family, Charles Fraser inherited honourable Jacobite traditions, which were to become a great influence on his own contributions to public life and private historical research in his later years. At first, he embarked on a legal career, entering the law office of John Mackay of Inverness in 1842, at the age of 14. In 1849 he went to Edinburgh University to continue his legal training and studies, studying Civil and Scots Law, Conveyancing, and Rhetoric. In 1853, at the age of only 25, he started up in business in Inverness and soon had a large and lucrative practice. He became assistant to the Sheriff Clerk, and then Procurator.

In 1857 he took his first dip into local politics when he supported the Liberal candidate, Alexander Campbell of Monzie, in the Parliamentary election for the Inverness Burghs against the Whig sitting member, Alexander Matheson of Ardross. The Whigs retained the seat, as they also did in 1859. On balance, these results were probably beneficial for Inverness, in that Sir Alexander Matheson, as he later became, worked tirelessly for the prosperity of Inverness; while not a brilliant politician, he was extremely hard-working, and through his own considerable financial investment coupled with considerable business acumen he contributed much to the development and improvement of Inverness, through his redevelopment of the west side of the river and his involvement with the Highland Railway.

In the same year that the young Charles Fraser was dabbling in politics his maternal uncle, Aeneas Mackintosh, died, stipulating in his will that if his nephew were to change his surname by adding Mackintosh to it, he would become a major beneficiary of his estate. Thus Charles Fraser-Mackintosh came into existence at the age of 29, and in due time a Royal Licence was obtained to ratify his new nomenclature.

His appetite whetted by this skirmish in national politics, Charles Fraser-Mackintosh was elected as a Town Councillor in Inverness in November 1857. He was re-elected in 1859 and again in 1861, but on 10 May 1862 he suddenly resigned, citing the pressures of business and health difficulties caused by overwork, and he retired completely from public life.

We now know that he was about to embark on a scheme which was both going to transform the town centre of Inverness and make his fortune. Along with three associates (George Grant Mackay, Donald Davidson and Hugh Rose) he embarked on the redesign of the area between the Railway Station and Church Street, which was a confusing network of old houses, workshops, closes and narrow lanes. The old buildings were purchased by the consortium and cleared away, and the work of building Union Street began. By 1864 the new street was finished, and from the first every office, shop and set of apartments was fully let.

Charles Fraser-Mackintosh and his three friends were the first to realise that the arrival of the railway in Inverness would lead to the expansion of the town and the growth of commerce and industry. There was plenty of room for the town to expand. It was surrounded by open fields, but only a few citizens seemed to be aware of the opportunities available. In 1863 Charles Fraser-Mackintosh bought the Drummond Estate, once the property of his relative Provost Phineas Mackintosh, and laid it out for feuing – that is, subjected it

Aerial view of Eastgate showing the railway station and auction mart.

to a process of subdivision and town planning which involved the creation of new streets and property boundaries, and the creation of property divisions which people were then invited to purchase and build on, while still paying an annual fee, or 'feu duty' to the owner of the land on which the houses were to be built. In 1860 he repeated the exercise on the estate of Ballifeary, on the west side of the river to the south of Matheson's holdings.

The further history of the expansion and development of Inverness is beyond the scope of this book, as is the future political career of Charles Fraser-Mackintosh. He was finally elected to Parliament in 1874 and served as the MP for the Inverness Burghs, and then for Inverness-shire, until 1892. He was the only Gaelic-speaking MP and in the 1880s served on the Napier Commission, which reported in 1884 and resulted in the Crofters Act of 1886. In later years he devoted himself to historical writing; it is generally reckoned that he was an excellent Victorian antiquarian but a poor historian. He was one of the foremost proponents of a free public library in Inverness and was involved in the opening ceremony at the new building in Castle Wynd, on 16 June 1883. He died on 25 January 1901, his tributes and obituaries unfortunately taking second place to those for Queen Victoria, who died on 22 January.

CHAPTER 8

INVERNESS BRIDGES

At the time of the opening of the Friar's Bridge, in 1987, there was some discussion in the local press about one of the prophecies of the Brahan Seer, to the effect that when the ninth bridge over the Ness was completed, something drastic would happen in the town.

Alexander Mackenzie first published *The Prophecies of the Brahan Seer* in 1899, with more than a hint of millennialist foreboding. He drew on oral traditions, which he collected together from various sources, and on the small amount of printed material which others had produced over the years. Mackenzie quoted the 'prophecies' as best he could, and gave his own commentary and interpretations. His book was reprinted in 1970 and is easily available to the modern reader.

Unfortunately, his work does not bear very close scrutiny. Elizabeth Sutherland, in *Ravens and Black Rain* (1985), showed that either Coinneach Odhar lived to be a very, very old man indeed, or else the 'prophecies' attributed to him were in fact either folk traditions from various sources, or actual prophecies and sayings by more than one person.

The prophecy concerning the bridges of Inverness is given (by Mackenzie) as follows:

> When two false teachers shall come across the seas who will revolutionise the religion of the land, and nine bridges shall span the river Ness, the Highlands will be overrun by ministers without grace and women without shame.

Alexander Mackenzie thought, in 1899, that this was 'a prediction which some maintain has all the appearance of being rapidly fulfilled at this moment'. Certainly there are plenty in Inverness today, over one hundred years on, who would argue that there are far more 'ministers without grace' and 'women without shame' in the Highland fleshpots now than there ever were before! In Mackenzie's time it was suggested that the 'two false teachers' from overseas were none other than Moody and Sankey, the American evangelists;

it is difficult to know who today's equivalents might be. Mackenzie calculated that the eighth bridge across the Ness had been completed the previous year, and that the ninth was nearing completion. He could not resist adding a few comments of his own:

> If we are to accept the opinions of certain of the clergy themselves, 'ministers without grace' are becoming the rule, and as for a plenitude of 'women without shame', ask any ancient matron, and she will at once tell you that Kenneth's prophecy may be held to have been fulfilled in that particular any time within the last half century. *Gleidh sinne*!!

Save us, indeed! Mackenzie's two exclamation marks do hint at a little ambiguity as to whether or not he really feared 'women without shame'!

However, when we start to compile a list of all the known bridges over the river Ness, it appears that the prophecy may have been fulfilled, if at all, some time ago:

1411	wooden bridge, 'the famousest and finest off oak in Brittain', destroyed by Donald of Harlaw
1620	replacement wooden bridge destroyed in flood
1624	timber bridge built: it fell down in 1664 and was not replaced for twenty-one years
1685	stone bridge of seven arches built, using stone from Cromwell's Fort
1808	Black Bridge built, of timber (replaced 1896)
1829	bridge from Ness Bank to Ness Islands
1834	bridge from Ness Islands to Bught. The stone bridge, and the two Ness Islands bridges, were all washed away in the great flood of 25 January 1849
1849	temporary wooden bridge constructed
1853	one Ness Islands bridge replaced
1853	second Ness Islands bridge replaced
1855	main Suspension Bridge opened on 23 August
1863	Railway Bridge built: it collapsed in 1989
1877	Infirmary Bridge built
1882	Greig Street Bridge built

1896   Waterloo Bridge opened, 26 February

1939   contract for a new granite bridge to replace the Suspension Bridge; temporary wooden bridge built a few yards upstream

1959   Suspension Bridge of 1855 closed; temporary bridge built

1961   new concrete bridge opened on 28 September

1982   Kessock Bridge opened in August – not strictly over the river Ness!

1987   Friars' Bridge opened

1990   replacement railway bridge

A total of twenty bridges, not counting the Kessock Bridge! Perhaps we are safe from Coinneach Odhar's prophecies?

There has been a ferry at Kessock since the fifteenth century. It was in private ownership and changed hands many times up to 1939, when it was taken over by local authorities. During the Second World War the *Lowestoft Belle* operated the service, followed by two small passenger boats, the *St Mawes* and the *Hope*. Eventually two boats, capable of carrying cars, were acquired, the *Eilean Dubh* (6 cars) and then in 1967 the *Rosehaugh*, built at Berwick and capable of carrying 28 cars and 150 passengers. A back-up vessel, the *Glenachulish* (6 cars) was also used.

Work began on the Kessock Bridge in April 1978 and it opened to traffic on 19 July 1982. It cost just £18 million. It was opened formally by the Queen Mother on 6 August 1982. Both the *Eilean Dubh* and the *Rosehaugh* made special farewell appearances – 'a part of a life now gone', according to Mr George Finlayson, Convenor of Ross and Cromarty District Council.

CHAPTER 9

POPULATION AND HOUSING

Population figures show the dramatic growth of the population of Inverness in the last half of the nineteenth century. Figures before the decennial census began in 1831 are inevitably estimates. Pennant (1769) had reckoned the population at around 11,000, while the Rev. James Hall (1803) thought it was around 6,000. Official census returns produce the following statistics:

1831	9,633
1841	11,592
1851	12,793
1861	12,509
1871	14,469
1881	17,385
1891	20,855

In 1891, of the population of 20,855, 6,356 were Gaelic speakers and 11,113 were women. There were 4,566 inhabited houses in the town. One hundred years later, the population of 'Inverness Settlement Zone' in the 1991 census was 41,766, to which the new estates around Smithton, Culloden and Balloch added a further 8,728, making a total of 50,494. Today the population exceeds 60,000, and is growing.

SQUATTERS

Housing shortages were a big problem in post-war Britain, and in this regard Inverness was no exception. Ex-servicemen, especially those who had been wounded or disabled, were particularly aggrieved, and matters came to a head in the summer of 1946, in Inverness as in many other parts of the country. The principle manifestation of discontent was the appearance of 'squatters', who occupied former War Department huts and buildings. About forty-one families in Inverness occupied sites at the Longman Aerodrome, Raigmore Wood, Annfield Road, Porterfield Road, and Muirtown. All were ex-servicemen, many with small children. The largest squatter colony was at the Longman site, where twenty families moved into huts recently vacated by the Air Ministry. Sanitary conditions there were poor.

At Raigmore, at the end of August, six families moved into huts owned by the Air Ministry, empty since November 1945, including ten children ranging in ages from fifteen months to nine years. One of the families had been waiting for a house for nine years. Not all of the empty huts were occupied at once, and some wrote their names and addresses on notices which were pinned to the doors, to reserve huts for future occupancy. One of the Porterfield huts was occupied by a family who had been living in a tent in the Haugh district because they could not get a house of their own from the Council.

The squatters attracted a lot of sympathy throughout the town. Many thought that the empty huts should have been used long before as a temporary remedy during the housing shortage, and Council employees offered to make some of the huts more habitable, by connecting lighting and improving sanitary arrangements. Many of the squatters let it be known that they were willing to pay rent, and they hoped that they would be allowed to stay, and that the government would find some way to legalise their position.

Two years later they were still there. In December 1948, just before Christmas, the Secretary of State for Scotland was successful in getting eviction orders against six of the Raigmore squatters. Meanwhile, the Town Council had been addressing the problem of housing and had made a start on two new housing 'schemes', at Dalneigh and Hilton. The Dalneigh Housing Site was the first to be started, and over the next five years was steadily extended. A feature of the new housing estate was the new 'Swedish' houses, purchased directly from Swedish suppliers in prefabricated form, and assembled in Inverness. At a sitting of the Inverness Dean of Guild Court (the planning authority) on 7 January 1946 permission was granted to the Scottish Special Housing Association to erect sixty-four permanent houses 'of the Swedish type' at Dalneigh, and at a meeting of the Housing Committee of the Town Council on the same night it was agreed to erect 'aluminium houses' at sites on Harrowden Road, Coronation Park, Bruce Avenue, Ballifeary Road and Culduthel Road.

Public opinion was sceptical: a correspondent calling himself 'Hope Deferred' wrote to the *Courier* in June 1946 that local housing policy seemed to be 'in a stupid and foolish muddle'. The Council had started building twenty houses in Bruce Gardens in November 1944, but they would not be ready until November 1946, and perhaps not even then. In August 1946 the Inverness Trades and Labour Council protested to the Secretary of State in the strongest possible terms about the delay in providing housing.

The Burgh Surveyor, Mr I. W. Jack, reported in June 1946 that the total cost of schemes under construction was £57,250, which would provide 650 new houses. By January 1948 the Burgh Architect, Mr J. Blackburn, was able to report progress: thirty-two houses were rapidly approaching completion at Hilton, where at the end of 1946 no house-building at all had been commenced, and at Dalneigh, 64 Swedish houses were finished. By mid November 1948 Mr Blackburn was able to report the purchase of a further 100 Swedish houses, to be erected at Dalneigh beginning in the spring of 1949.

However, in November 1949 the Town Council's Housing Committee had to address the difficult question of housing allocation for the Swedish houses. The 'economic' rent for a Swedish house worked out at about £65 a year, and as one Councillor pointed out, there was no point in allocating such a house to an ordinary working man earning £5 a week if he would have to pay £2 a week in rent and rates. The proposed solution was to move council tenants with a higher income into the newer houses, and allow those with a lower income to occupy existing housing. In due time, the names and addresses of the successful tenants for the new houses in the Hilton and Dalneigh schemes were published in the local press for all to see. At last, it was possible to proclaim Inverness free of 'squatters' and to demolish superfluous military huts.

In *The Hub of the Highlands* (1975), the comprehensive 'Book of Inverness' published by the Inverness Field Club, there is an interesting contribution by Frank Spaven, then Chief Planning Officer for the Highlands and Islands Development Board and also Chairman of the Inverness Civic Trust, founded in 1967. He was at pains to point out that 'development' and 'conservation' did not have to be enemies:

If "development" is regarded rather as an unfolding and promotion of the use of the latent resources of a place and its people and "conservation" as a husbanding of these resources for sustained use, the two can be seen to be complementary processes and agencies for living, the one more active and the other more passive, each a necessary partner to the other.

He worried about the ever-increasing influx of tourists into Inverness, and the lack of adequate infrastructure to handle them, including issues of traffic management and transport links. He described Inverness as a 'mixter-maxter' of a town, contrasting the preservation of historic buildings with the undisputed need for large buildings desperately needed to provide services to the population: the telephone exchange, large modern hotels, a new, large modern hospital. His crystal ball was not perfect, but his thoughts are as apt today as they were thirty-five years ago:

> It is suggested that development and conservation are not opposed but complementary aspects of growth in the Inverness district; that, when their promoters have worked together and with planners, there has been a successful outcome, especially in the countryside and in physical planning for industry; that the impact of road transport on towns and villages is a striking failure in this respect; that the buildings of large, urban institutions are also difficult to cope with; that the rapid pace of oil-related growth is creating shortages and inflations which are not yet under control; and that tourism is likely to move in the direction of more control and steering of development.

> Nothing has been said here about the important, but intangible, question of conserving community life and values. Yet Inverness has always been a meeting place of Highland and Lowland people and ideas. It is well used to absorbing incomers, and it should be better able to continue doing so in conditions of oil and tourism boom than smaller, more isolated communities farther to the west and north.

CHAPTER 10

PHOTOGRAPHIC COLLECTIONS

Pierre Delavault must have relied to a great extent on earlier visual records of important buildings and townscapes around Inverness. We are fortunate in having the David Whyte Collection and the Joseph Cook Collection of early photographs, documenting the visual appearance of Inverness from the 1890s onwards. Now in the Highland Photographic Archive, under the care of the Highland Council, many of the hundreds of glass plates have been digitised and appear on the council's Am Baile website, administered by Highland Libraries. We are pleased to be able to reproduce a selection of these early photographs in this book. Copies of material in the Highland Photographic Archive can be ordered, at a price, through Am Baile.

JOSEPH COOK (1880–1973)

Joseph Cook was the son of Robert Cook and Mary Walker and was born in Inverness on 14 October 1880. He attended the Inverness Royal Academy before joining the family firm, James Walker & Co., timber merchants, whose premises were at the Shore. During World War I he was a captain in the Cameron Highlanders and before being demobbed he worked for the forestry service. He married Catherine (Kate) Munro Bookless, daughter of James Bookless, a fishmonger with a business in Union Street. The marriage took place at her parents' house on 20 November 1915. On the death of his father Joseph became manager of the sawmill and held the post for 65 years.

He was a founder member of the Inverness Rotary Club, a manager of the Inverness Savings Bank, a deacon in the Free Church and, for 50 years, was a member of the Inverness Harbour Trust. He was also a keen amateur historian and gave lectures with lantern slides, as well as amassing a large collection of photographs of Inverness and its surroundings. A series of articles which he wrote for the *Inverness Courier* appear in his book, *The Port of*

Inverness, published in 1931. He was also a self-taught dry-point etcher and two of his plates, 'Off Cromarty' and 'Avoch Fishing Boats', were bought by a firm of London art publishers.

He and his wife lived first at 7 Muirfield Road before building a new house in the garden which became number 15. He and his wife were also interested in the Highland Orphanage and Kate ran sewing parties to make clothes for the children. The couple had no children of their own, but during World War II they took in Charles Massey, an evacuee, and later adopted him. They celebrated their Golden Wedding in 1965.

Kate died in 1966 and Joseph in 1973. He was 92. He is described in his obituary as being 'amiable with a charming manner and possessing a great, if not to say, pawky sense of humour'.

His collection of photographs was donated to Inverness Museum and Art Gallery and many of them are available to view on Am Baile.

DAVID WHYTE (1841–1905)

The self-styled 'Leading Photographer of the North' came to Inverness from his native Ayr in the 1860s and established a photographic business in the town. His first premises were in Greig Street, but he soon outgrew these and moved in quick succession to premises in Huntly Street, then to Union Street. In 1870 he purchased the business of his rivals, Messrs Collier & Park, at 18 Church Street. His final move, sometime in the 1870s, took him a few doors down to 57 Church Street, and there the business remained until 1985. The well-lit photographic studio on the top floor is now occupied by the Workers' Educational Association (WEA).

The majority of his photographs were commissioned and include portraits of family groups, weddings and babies. Of particular interest to the social historian are the many photographs of shop windows and frontages.

After his death in 1905 his widow continued to operate the business for several more years. Subsequently, a succession of proprietors took over the business but maintained Whyte's name. It finally closed in 1985. The last proprietor, Mr F Hardley, deposited the vast collection of around 140,000 negatives and prints to the Highland Regional Council's Museums Service. They are now in the care of the Highland Photographic Archive.

I am grateful to Am Baile for providing information on Joseph Cook and David Whyte.

HIGH STREET, 1870

This view of the High Street in 1870 shows, on the right, the striking building then occupied by Grant's Tartan and Tweed Warehouse, catering to the
tourist trade and the sartorial needs of the gentry. It is surmounted by the
Three Virtues, who, after spending some time in a garden in Orkney, are now
back in Inverness. After restoration the Highland Council positioned this
municipal statuary on a ground-level plinth on Ness Bank, below the Castle,
allowing modern Invernessians to inspect their charms without craning their
necks. Representing Faith, Hope and Charity, the Three Virtues are not to be
confused with the Three Graces, the Greek goddesses of charm, beauty and
creativity. The statues were seven feet tall, the work of Inverness sculptor
Andrew Davidson (1841–1925). The building was demolished in 1955.

The taxi cabs in the foreground are waiting for passing trade in Exchange
Square, in front of what is now the Town House.

MacDougall's Tartan Warehouse, High Street

This illustration of MacDougall's Tartan Warehouse, at 23 High Street, is taken from Alexander Mackenzie's *Guide to Inverness* (1893). This emporium appealed shamelessly to the Victorians' love of tartan and tweed, satisfying all the indoor and outdoor clothing needs of the Victorian gentry. The three-storey baronial style building dates from 1878–79, and is by the architects Matthews and Lawrie.

Bridge Street, 1959–60

This view of Bridge Street (opposite, top) was taken around 1959–60, just before this part of the town centre was demolished to make way for the concrete boxes of Inverness Museum and the Crofters Commission which have attracted so much criticism. The buildings in this picture are not pretty, are a bit haphazard, hint at severely overcrowded housing, and perhaps were not seriously lamented when they were demolished.

The architectural 'crime' of the redevelopment of Bridge Street in the 1960s lay not so much in the demolitions of 'traditional' buildings, as in the

Bridge Street, 1959–60.

wholly unimaginative, soulless structures which arose in their place. Yet, in their time, those concrete excrescences, as they are now viewed, were seen as the latest thing in urban architecture.

BRIDGE STREET, LOOKING NORTH

Viewed from the bottom of Bridge Street, from the riverside, this shows why the planners were so keen to demolish all the buildings on the right of the photograph and widen the street. The traffic was a menace to pedestrians and cyclists; construction of the new bridge was under way – one of the workers' huts is just visible in the right of this photo, on the site of the already demolished buildings known as Castle Tolmie. The buildings on the left were demolished too, at least as far as the cars, including 'Queen Mary's House'.

QUEEN MARY'S HOUSE

This photograph of 'Queen Mary's House', shortly before its demolition in 1968, shows why the planners got it so wrong. There was a good case for widening Bridge Street to accommodate modern traffic conditions, and the buildings on the south side of the street were largely dispensable. However, this house, dating in part from the sixteenth century, should have been preserved. In an ultimate irony, it was demolished to make way for the headquarters of the Highlands and Islands Development Board, which, with perhaps an exaggerated sense of their own importance, decided to occupy what is arguably the prime site in Inverness for their own purposes.

The late medieval buildings were much altered in 1787 by William Inglis of Kingsmills. He remodelled the first and second floors but kept the thick ground-floor walls of the original structure. The house takes its name from events in 1562, when the army of Mary, Queen of Scots laid siege to Inverness Castle. It was occupied by Alexander Gordon, the Earl of Huntly's Lieutenant-Governor, but with assistance from Frasers and Mackintoshes the castle was captured and Gordon was hanged. Local tradition asserts that Mary occupied this house while she was in Inverness.

The continuing irony of this site is that HIDB, mutating into Highlands and Islands Enterprise (HIE), found their concrete building both unsatisfactory and too small, moving to a new office building on the eastern outskirts of Inverness, leaving their erstwhile showpiece to be converted to flats.

There seemed to be a possibility in the 1990s that a purpose-built cultural complex might be built in this area, incorporating library, archives, museum and art gallery facilities, with associated offices, auditoriums and display space, but such innovative ideas proved to be well beyond the imagination of councillors and planning officials.

From the late eighteenth century these buildings were occupied by Fraser, Wilson & Co., wine and spirit merchants. Vaults from the original buildings were incorporated into the redevelopment.

Advertisement for Mackintosh and Co. featuring Queen Mary's House.

Edward Meldrum, himself very interested in the architectural history of Inverness and the author of a small guidebook, took a number of photographs of Queen Mary's House before its demolition.

Photograph by Edward Meldrum of the coat of arms on the wall of Queen Mary's House.

Queen Mary's House seen through the gateway of the bridge (Edward Meldrum).

Basement of Queen Mary's House (Edward Meldrum).

THE OLD TOWN HOUSE

This is the Old Town House, built in 1708 as the town house of Lord Lovat. It became the administrative headquarters for the Burgh in 1716 and was demolished in 1878 to make way for the splendid Town House, which fortunately survived the depredations of the 1960s.

Also located in this building were reading rooms where local gentlemen could consult newspapers and magazines, or perhaps read the books comprising the 'Kirk Session' library – effectively the library of the medieval burgh, later placed in the care of the church authorities. These books, which are little read today, are now stored in the public library at Farraline Park, under the care of Highland Libraries.

In front of the Old Town House is The Exchange, where public proclamations, as for example at the death of a monarch, were traditionally made, at the Market Cross. There, too, the Clachnacuddin Stone was venerated. 'The Stone of the Tubs', reputedly taking its name from the custom of women resting their washing tubs there on their way to and from the river, is of unknown origin.

DEMOLITION OF THE OLD TOWN HOUSE

This shot of the demolition of the Old Town House, taken by Joseph Cook in 1878, shows some of the adjacent buildings in Exchange Place and Castle Street at that time.

THE EXCHANGE, FORBES FOUNTAIN

The Forbes Fountain (previous page) was placed in front of the Town House to commemorate Dr Forbes, hero and victim of the cholera epidemics which swept through Inverness in the 1830s. It was presented to the council in 1880 by Dr George F. Forbes of Millburn. Removed by the Council for 'safe-keeping' during the demolitions of the 1960s, it was stored in a council yard. Subsequently some surviving fragments were erected near the War Memorial at Cavell Gardens, on Ladies' Walk.

Huntly Street in the 1950s

This postcard of the view from Huntly Street shows the suspension bridge, demolished in 1959, and the original Caledonian Hotel.

Exchange Place

Dating from 1959–60, this photograph (opposite, bottom) shows what is now called Castle Wynd, but was originally known as Exchange Place – the building to the left of the picture is the Town House. The buildings to the left of the shops were occupied by the public library and museum – after reconstruction the library continued there, before moving to Farraline Park. Cairngorm House was a jeweller's shop.

CASTLE ROAD

This picture was taken during the construction of the new bridge over the River Ness, replacing the suspension bridge which had become unsuitable for modern traffic. On the left are huts built for the construction workers. The suspension bridge dated from 1855, replacing the stone bridge swept away by floods in 1849. It was originally planned to build a new bridge in 1938 and a temporary structure was begun then, but plans were interrupted by war in 1939. The war years only underlined the need for a new bridge, as military traffic placed intolerable demands on the existing infrastructure in the town centre.

The workers' huts are on the site of Castle Tolmie, demolished in 1959 at the same time as the suspension bridge. A temporary road bridge, visible in this photograph, was put in place and the new bridge was opened in 1961.

THE NESS BRIDGE

With a span of 225 ft, the main Ness Bridge provided a fitting entrance to the town from 1855 until its demolition in 1959. There was a large, imposing battlemented archway at the east side, with two smaller towers at the west end. Across the road from the archway, at the foot of Bridge Street, were the buildings known as Castle Tolmie.

TOWN HOUSE CAR PARK, CASTLE STREET

This view (opposite, top), from around 1960, of the Town House car park on Castle Street, shows the buildings on Exchange Place (renamed as Castle Wynd) and Bridge Street, which were demolished in the 1960s. The building on Exchange Place nearest to the car park was built in the 1880s to accommodate the new Free Public Library and the Museum. The car park came into being as a result of landslides in the 1930s which damaged existing housing on Castle Street, which had to be demolished.

The most serious landslide on Castle Street took place on Saturday 8 October 1932 when the retaining wall between the Castle and the houses on the west side of the street collapsed. About a month earlier a police inspector had reported cracks in the wall, and just the day before the collapse a local technical expert had examined the site – and decided to call in a yet more senior expert. Meanwhile, nobody thought to warn the residents. Nobody was killed but several people were treated for shock. The night before, 200 children had been in the new Mission Hall of St Columba's church, opened just a few months earlier. It was totally destroyed in the landslide. It was

Town House Car Park, Castle Street.

thought that the collapsed wall had been built by General Wade in the 1720s as part of the plan to build a barracks block at Inverness Castle. The edge of the landslide was only a few feet away from the foundations of the castle.

In the background is the steeple of the Tolbooth, on Bridge Street.

CASTLE STREET

This photograph (previous page) of Castle Street shows the back of buildings, mostly very dense housing, which were demolished in the 1930s following landslides on that side of the castle mound. The statue in the foreground in front of the castle, of Flora MacDonald, was designed by Andrew Davidson, a sculptor from Inverness.

Esso Station on Millburn Road

Petrol stations come and go and are amongst our most ephemeral structures. This Esso outlet was on Millburn Road – the buildings survive as the Farm & Household Stores, though the petrol pumps and kiosk are long gone. The garage belonged to J. Ferries & Co. Fortunately the price per gallon cannot be deciphered.

The Junction of Millburn Road and Crown Road

This photograph (opposite, top) from the 1950s shows the junction of Millburn Road and Crown Road and the premises of R. S. MacDonald & Company, a tailor's shop. This whole area of Inverness was extensively demolished in 1983 for the construction of the Eastgate Centre, a modern shopping mall.

The junction of Millburn Street and Crown Road.

BANK STREET AND THE CALEDONIAN HOTEL

The Caledonian Hotel was demolished in 1968, bringing to an end an era of opulence and luxury unsurpassed anywhere in the Highlands. The original buildings dated from 1780, built as a meeting place for members of the St John's Masonic Lodge – and known then as the Masons' Hotel or the Mason Lodge Hotel, until it was renamed as the Caledonian Hotel in 1825. Reputedly the funds for the original building came from the Commissioners of Forfeited Estates – the government body which administered the estates confiscated from people who had supported the Jacobites during the 1745–46 Rising.

The building was enlarged in 1822 and 1882 and was famous for its ballroom. Royalty and aristocracy made it the place to stay in the Highland capital. The current hotel on this site represents the failure of imagination so typical of redevelopment in Inverness in the 1960s and 1970s.

The 'back' entrance of the Caledonian Hotel on Church Street maintains its quality and splendour. In Alexander Mackenzie's 1893 guidebook it is described as 'the only First-Class Hotel overlooking the River Ness.'

THE SUSPENSION BRIDGE, BANK STREET

Almost all the buildings visible in this picture (opposite, top) were demolished in the 1960s, with the notable exception of the *Inverness Courier* offices on the left of this picture. The Editor, Miss Barron, held out against the local planning bullies and the building she refused to sell stands today as a monument to one individual's rebellion against 'progress'.

The suspension bridge.

The suspension bridge was demolished in 1959–60. The Town Steeple, originally part of the town's gaol and courthouse, survives despite being damaged by an earthquake in 1816.

THE *COURIER* OFFICE

Occupied by the *Inverness Courier* since 1838, only in recent years did the newspaper close its town offices when it moved to its new premises, Century House, beneath the Kessock Bridge. The building is now occupied by Strutt and Parker, estate agents.

Union Street

This engraving of Union Street in the 1870s is from *Invernessiana* (1875), by Charles Fraser-Mackintosh.

Dalcross's House, Queensgate

Dalcross's House (opposite, top), at the corner of Queensgate and Church Street, was demolished to make way for a branch of the Clydesdale Bank. The carved stones above the dormers were preserved. In this photograph (opposite, bottom), dating from the 1870s, the shop on the corner with rabbits or hares hanging above the windows is George MacLeod, Fishmonger and Poulterer. The house was built in 1700.

Queensgate Post Office

The original Queensgate Post Office (opposite, bottom) was built in 1888, designed by Alexander Ross in the Italianate style, using sandstone. It

Top: Dalcross's House, Queensgate.
Bottom: Queensgate Post Office.

opened in 1890 but suffered earthquake damage in November of that year. It was demolished in the 1960s to make way for the current woeful concrete structure.

THE ORIGINAL INVERNESS POST OFFICE

This drawing shows the original Inverness Post Office, opened in 1840 on the corner of Church Street and Bank Lane.

THE PICTURE PALACE/EMPIRE THEATRE

The Central Hall Picture House, the Picture Palace (opposite), by Alexander Ross & Son, architects, opened on Academy Street in 1912. It was redesigned in 1934 and renamed as the Empire Theatre. The building closed in 1970 and was demolished in 1971.

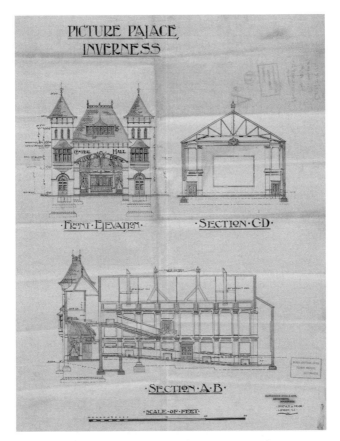

Top: architects' plan of the Picture Palace.
Bottom: the Picture Palace in its new guise as the Empire Theatre.

RAINING'S STAIRS

In 1726 John Raining, a merchant from Norwich, bequeathed £1,200 to establish a fund to support charitable schools in the Highlands. The trust was administered by the Society for the Propagation of Christian Knowledge, who built a three-storey school at the end of Ardconnel Street in 1757. Extensions were added in 1840 and 1881, but by 1894 the pupils had been transferred to the nearby High School. The building was demolished in 1976. Raining's Stairs, named to commemorate the benefactor, led from Ardconnel Street to Castle Street.

This photograph, from the Joseph Cook Collection, shows dense housing on both sides of the stone stairs. The building at the bottom of the stairs, on the other side of Castle Street, is part of the Town House now housing local council offices.

RAINING'S SCHOOL

Raining's School, latterly known as the **YWCA** building, was well known to generations of Invernessians as a venue for dances and meetings of clubs and societies.

CHAPTER 11

BRIDGE STREET

In seeking to understand how it came about that so many important buildings were demolished in Bridge Street in the 1960s, it is instructive to examine the coverage of events in the *Inverness Courier*. The Editor, Miss Barron, never made any secret of her own opinions in numerous editorials, but the news coverage of events as they developed does give an idea of the apparently inevitable march of progress.

Things started off in a reasonably uncontentious way. There was widespread agreement that the Suspension Bridge, the main bridge over the Ness at the historic crossing point below the Castle, needed to be replaced. Everything had been agreed and put into motion in 1937, just before the war, even to the extent of building a temporary bridge, at a cost of £4,530. With the outbreak of war in 1939 these plans were put on hold, but the tremendous increase in traffic during the war years, as the result of military activities, made it almost unanimous that a new bridge was required. Nobody could have imagined that it would be another 20 years before anything happened, but post-war Britain was an impoverished and debt-laden society and there were many other priorities.

Tenders for the construction contract for the new bridge had to be lodged with the Town Council by 8 June 1959. The original estimate of costs for the whole project, including demolition of the existing bridge and associated reconstruction of roads, walls and pavements, was £129,000. By 1959 this estimate had risen to just over £250,000. The Town Council had hoped for a 100% grant from central government, but the Roads Division of the Scottish Home Department had offered only 75%.

Regulations pertaining to traffic management measures surrounding the new scheme came into effect on 1 September 1959, causing great confusion for motorists. From that date, the Suspension Bridge was closed and two-way traffic came into effect on the strengthened temporary bridge. A further temporary footbridge was also planned. A local Esso dealer attempted (unsuccessfully) to help its customers by publishing a map of the new arrangements.

Pipers marching to the Highland Games over the Suspension Bridge.

The Town Council was not minded to let the closure of the old bridge take effect without suitable observances:

> Last night members of the Town Council, watched by a cheerful, good-natured crowd of almost a thousand townspeople, marched across the Suspension Bridge at midnight to the strains of the bagpipe tune, the Slow March "Mo Dachaidh" ("My Home").
>
> Earlier in the day it had been agreed, at a meeting of the Town Council Works Committee, on the motion of Councillor Donald Urquhart, that the closing of the old bridge should be officially recognised, and shortly before midnight members of the Town Council and officials, headed by Mr Calum Macdonald, Bar Officer at The Castle, playing "The 79th's Farewell to Gibraltar," and Mr Charles Macrae, Town Officer, marched from the Exchange to the archway of the Bridge. Accompanying them was Mr Roderick Macdonald, son of the late Sir Murdoch Macdonald, M.P., who is a principal of the firm, Sir Murdoch Macdonald and Partners, the consulting engineers for the bridge scheme. In the rear of the municipal party was Councillor William Campbell, riding a motor-cycle combination, and he thus had the distinction of being the last to drive a vehicle over the bridge before it was legally closed to traffic. All along Bridge Street, at the entrance to the bridge, and on the bridge itself people lined the route.

At the entrance to the archway, when the Councillors halted, Bailie Jack Fraser, Senior Bailie, in the absence of Provost Robert Wotherspoon, who is in the South, made a brief speech, declaring that it was an historic occasion for the town, for a bridge which had been a faithful servant for 104 years, an old friend of them all, was to be demolished. He wished the engineers and contractors every success in their undertaking.

Police had some difficulty clearing the roadway of the bridge for the municipal party to cross, but once the Councillors got under way – whether they were out of step it was difficult to see as the bridge was in darkness – the crowd fell in behind, and made the crossing for the last time.

At the west end of the bridge the pipes broke into "The Inverness Gathering," and the Councillors, with a more jaunty step, turned into Ness Walk, and returned by way of the Temporary Bridge, while some people made their first crossing of the river by the new footbridge alongside.

To mark this occasion the *Courier* took the opportunity to give its readers a potted history of previous bridges, noting that the Suspension Bridge replaced the late seventeenth century stone bridge of seven arches, swept away in the great flood of Thursday, 25 January 1849 – 'at exactly quarter-past six on the Thursday morning.'

Bridge Street houses below Castle Hill, 1959.

The successful contractors were Messrs Duncan Logan (Contractors) Ltd., of Muir of Ord. They quickly decided not to demolish the old bridge immediately, as it provided useful access for their construction equipment. Mr Duncan Logan himself took charge as a mobile crane was set up to excavate the river bed, watched carefully by townspeople from the river banks.

In that first week of September 1959 the *Courier* printed some letters from readers, including one from Thomas C. Hendrie in Glasgow, who was the grandson of John Hendrie, the builder of the Suspension Bridge – and also 'St Andrew's Cathedral; the Caledonian Bank; one-half of Union Street; the Highland Railway buildings and workshops; Ellon Castle, Aberdeenshire; and all the stations on the Dingwall and Kyle of Lochalsh Railway line.' An anonymous writer thought that perhaps the imposing stone archway of the old bridge could be preserved and re-erected at the Bruce Gardens entrance to Tomnahurich Cemetery.

It is fair to say that there was minimal public opposition to these developments, but another anonymous letter-writer made some prescient observations:

> The civic heads of Inverness, to their credit, afforded the doomed Suspension Bridge a farewell ceremony that was simple and moving. It struck the right note, though some say the success of the affair was due to the fact that the Council were given no time to think. The planners, thank Heaven, were denied the chance to indulge their wondrous imaginations, and we were spared, therefore, fireworks, searchlights, massed infantry, and Macnamara's band. There was some bickering and indecision ere the dignified goodbye was sanctioned, but so what? Isn't it obvious, in the aftermath, that the proposed prostituting of the bridge's last hours in the name of always-present good causes (tourist industry and younger generation) would have been shameful and shabby? Surely for a bridge that has stood for 104 years we did right in putting aside all thoughts of "making a killing?"

> And so the red tower stands alone now, in this the last summer of its long life. There is no suggestion of unsteadiness; rather it has an air of permanence. It could stand for another 100 years, but it does not belong in this age of the bubble car, the philosophy of the paper cup and the "scrubbing brush" haircut – it is condemned. Like Castle Tolmie and the old Y.M.C.A. building, the red tower will soon be no more. Next on the list, apparently, is the "Bell's School."

All that is Inverness, in the way of sticks and stones, is being systematically wiped out. I am beginning to wonder if such brutality is not being overdone.

    – Yours etc, ONLOOKER.

Early in October, L. P. Murray offered up a poem 'To The Bridge', of which we will inflict on the reader only the first and last stanzas:

> Thou Bridge, on whose suspended span
> Has trod that various creature man.
> For many long decades now old
> And many purposes untold
> Whose form at last the fates decree
> Must very shortly cease to be . . .
>
> And so, we take our leave of thee,
> Companion of a century,
> Whose breaking-up will break a part
> Of every Invernessian heart.
> In thee the past we bid adieu
> And forward look to bridges new.

In that same week in October 1959 there came the first intimation of plans for the redevelopment of Bridge Street. Mr D. B. Grant, convener of the Inverness Works Committee, presided over a meeting at which it was 'recommended that development corporations should be invited, through advertising, to submit plans for the redevelopment of Bridge Street.' The Inverness Architectural Association had written to the Committee asking 'that the redevelopment be the subject of an open or limited competition between architects,' but this was not what Provost Wotherspoon had in mind. By 8 votes to 2 it was decided that only development corporations should be approached and asked to submit plans for the redevelopment. Only Bailie A. G. Pollitt and Mr Angus Fraser voted against – Gerald Pollitt was to become a real thorn in the side of the increasingly secretive Provost and Councillors as events unfolded.

By November 1959 Miss Barron had had enough. In a long and thoughtful editorial in the issue of 6 November, she noted that the Town Council had now invited development corporations to submit their ideas for the redevelopment of Bridge Street:

The south side of Bridge Street, 1960.

As it will be the most comprehensive scheme of town improvement within living memory, probably comparable in scale only to the construction of Union Street and Queensgate last century, considerable public interest has naturally been aroused in the project. The policy which the Town Council are adopting has, too, equally naturally, come in for some discussion not only in those business, professional and financial circles concerned with the building trade but also by the general public, some of whom are perturbed lest the Town Council are failing to make the most of the opportunity which the Bridge Street re-development presents.

Noting that Councillors were no doubt distracted by the recent General Election campaign, she declared that it was little wonder that there should be 'a good deal of uneasiness among the public in case the Council are acting somewhat rashly.' She raised the possibility of a new public hall and perhaps a new museum being part of the planning and concluded:

These and many other aspects of the reconstruction of Bridge Street deserve the most careful examination before anything of an irrevocable nature is done. Bridge Street is one of the oldest and most historic parts of the Highland Capital.

She also noted the likelihood that important historic and archaeological opportunities were likely to arise during the demolition and building operations. At this stage, only demolition of the south side of Bridge Street was contemplated.

The *Courier* returned to this theme at the end of November 1959, when the Town Council published its detailed Development Plan for the next twenty years:

> When one studies the Development Plan in detail, and reads about proposals to sweep away buildings in Millburn, Eastgate and the whole south side of High Street; to clear the way for the creation of boulevards on both sides of the River Ness; to drive new roads through residential property; and, as a very long-term policy, to demolish very good-class property in Academy Street to widen the thoroughfare to 64 feet, one is left wondering if the plan's outcome would be not so much the development of Inverness but the destruction of the Highland Capital as it exists to-day. Goodness knows, the town has many limitations, since it was not built for the modern motor age, but surely it is not necessary to knock it down in this wholesale fashion in order to improve it . . . It is all very well to talk airily of acquiring rows of business properties, demolishing buildings, and re-building on cleared sites, but would be much better really if the Council were devoting its energies towards the initiation and completion of projects which are urgently needed, and are within its capacity to carry out in the near future.

It is interesting to note that the planners, despite their unbridled imagination which so worried Miss Barron, got their demographics completely wrong, predicting that by 1979 the population would have risen to 33,000, an increase of only 5,000 in twenty years. There is a very full report on the Development Plan in the *Courier* for 27 November 1959. Copies could be purchased from the Council for £4.

Meanwhile, construction continued on the new bridge, and in the middle of December 1959 demolition of the main historic archway was begun.

The original deadline of 15 January for submitting plans for the redevelopment of Bridge Street was extended to 15 March, as prospective bidders commented on the complexity of what was proposed. 7 January 1960 was the last day for submitting objections to the Development Plan to the Secretary of State for Scotland. The Inverness Chamber of Commerce arranged a public meeting in the Town Hall to discuss things – the purpose of which, said their Vice-President Mr R. Morrison Smith, 'was not to object to the plan, but merely to clear up certain points, and to ensure as full a discussion as possible.' He was keen to suggest that questions from the audience 'should be of a general nature and not refer to specific and personal queries.'

When the meeting took place, it was a lively affair, and very well attended. The Burgh Architect, Jack Blackburn, had spent 11 years on the Development Plan, but only six weeks were available for public consultation, including the Christmas and New Year holidays. The Burgh Treasurer, W. J. Mackay, tried to explain that the Plan was flexible and still subject to alteration, but R. R. MacEwan, himself a former convener of Inverness Town Council's Planning Committee, pointed out the likely conflicts between the interests of a private developer and the interests of the local community. In a letter to the *Courier* he had warned that 'they have created a set of conditions which, if unchanged, will make it a near-certainty that the town centre will be spoilt for generations to come.' And Onlooker, in another contribution, suggested that "it may not have occurred to the planners that the tourist may find Inverness attractive because it's a little behind his own in modernity, the name for this being charm."

At the end of January 1960 the Inverness Architectural Association broke cover, in a letter to the *Courier* signed by its President, Ian A. Munro and eight professional colleagues: W. W. Mitchell, Alex Cullen, J. M. Lawrie, Alan D. McKillop, Alastair M. Grant, Kenneth J. Finlayson, Howard J. Chitty and A. McGraw. They pleaded for the Town Council to reconsider:

> It should surely be realised that the Bridge Street site, as viewed from the new bridge by visitors and citizens alike, will convey the character and dignity of the whole town of Inverness, and it is imperative that the whole project be developed in such a way as to ensure this end. We sincerely hope that it is still not too late for the Town Council to reconsider its decision as to the method of developing this key site, but if so, we trust that its members will have the good sense to call in an expert consultant to advise them on the "speculative" designs submitted. Immediate financial return should not be considered more important than the preservation of our natural heritage, and we strongly feel that if a speculative design is adopted for this project, regardless of appearance, the result will be a desecration of one of the principal viewpoints and attractions in Inverness.

Ian W. Jack, a former Burgh Surveyor, supported this plea. Dismissing the idea that they had left it too late, he endorsed their worries and concluded:

> The Council have a grave responsibility to the community. They are building not just for quick returns to-day but for posterity. They as paymen in such matters are in bounden duty on behalf of the citizens to take heed of expert professional advice. Further, the criterion in assessing the merits of any development scheme should not rest on either legal finesse or financial wizardry. It should be governed by considerations for the enhancement of the amenities and architectural dignity of our beautiful town – the Capital of the Highlands.

A special meeting of the Town Council was scheduled for 28 March, to consider eight competing schemes, with models, for the development of Bridge Street. In a foretaste of things to come, the Council voted 15–3 to hold the meeting in private, including viewing the architectural models. Only Gerald Pollitt, Dean of Guild Peter Ross and Bailie Ross voted for public proceedings, agreeing that private sessions would be needed to discuss commercial matters.

In the *Courier*, Miss Barron was incensed. In an editorial headed 'Bridge Street Secrecy,' appropriately published on 1 April 1960, she pulled no punches:

> It is not surprising that there is growing public concern about Inverness Town Council's policy in regard to the re-development of Bridge Street. For, judging by the secrecy and furtiveness in which the Council's actions have been shrouded, it would almost seem as if the Council imagine that they are dealing with their own private property, and not with buildings and sites which belong to the community.

She was, of course, scrupulously careful never to accuse anybody, in print, of corrupt behaviour, but this came close to crossing that legal line. Gathering a head of steam, she asserted:

> Of course, every reasonable person will agree that financial, and probably certain other, details of individual schemes and offers should not be disclosed at this stage, but nobody – not even the most

126

dictatorial or self-important Town Councillor – can dispute that the public, whom the Council, after all, are supposed to represent, are entitled to know every detail of the schemes, and who the offerers are, before any scheme is approved. The public interest is, or should be, the Council's paramount concern.

The Bridge Street development, moreover, will be the most comprehensive scheme of town improvement undertaken in Inverness for generations, and it is to be carried out in a manner befitting the town's historical heritage and modern needs, the Town Council must shed their reluctance to take the public into their confidence, and get it out of their heads that they can ride rough-shod over public opinion. Already the matter has attracted a great deal of publicity throughout, and beyond, Scotland, and it will attract a great deal more publicity – and of an adverse kind – if the Council do not depart from the hole-and-corner policy they have been pursuing. It is, indeed, quite preposterous of the present Town Council to think that they can deal with one of the oldest thoroughfares in Inverness as if it were no concern of the public.

They did not heed her warnings, including her prediction that a public inquiry and possible legal action would inevitably follow.

The controversy rumbled on throughout the rest of 1960, with the Council holding continued 'private sessions', or, as Miss Barron and most of her correspondents preferred, 'secret meetings'. Councillor Frank Rizza put pen to paper in the public press; Bailie Gerald Pollitt got into terrible trouble by being interviewed by BBC television for their 'Compass' programme. Provost Robert Wotherspoon was not pleased; neither he nor the Town Clerk (Mr James Cameron) had known about Bailie Pollitt's appearance. Worst of all, the *Highland News* had published transcripts of his comments. Bailie Pollitt defended himself, denying that he had breached any confidentiality. Writing in the *Courier*, Thomas D. Hood thought that Pollitt's remarks and opinions 'were amply justified'. At last, he wrote, 'we were seeing signs of someone unfettered on the Town Council' who was not 'a member of Inverness Secret Society – as those who adversely criticise Bailie Pollitt surely must be.' Another 'private session' was held on 14 May, voting 9–8 to exclude the public, so it is clear that public disquiet was starting to be noticed, at last.

'Another Secret Meeting' reported in July prompted another scathing editorial in the *Courier*: 'More Secrecy'. Finally, the Council's 'Planning Consultant', Mr Robert J. Naismith of Edinburgh, reported on the redevelopment schemes (and models) at the end of July. In September, six companies approved of by him were asked to re-submit revised schemes for Bridge Street; a motion by Mr Francesco ('Frank') Rizza to hold all future meetings in public was ruled 'incompetent' by Provost Wotherspoon.

The Council's paranoia over 'secrecy' spilled over into ridicule in December when yet another discussion of Bridge Street resulted in a defeat for the four Councillors wanting improved public access:

> Comical precautions were taken to ensure that there was no possibility of the waiting reporters hearing anything that was going on behind the closed doors of the Council Chamber. The door to the Press Gallery was locked – presumably in case some reporter sneaked in, and, unseen by the Councillors, heard the debate – and, lest any of them might listen outside the Press Gallery door, the reporters were not allowed near the entrance to the stairway leading to the Gallery. None of the reporters, of course, would have stooped to such conduct, and the secrecy precautions merely mirrored the minds of those responsible for them.
>
> Inside the Council Chamber were models of the Bridge Street Scheme, the apparent cause of all the secrecy, and when the pressmen were eventually admitted to the Chamber to get the statement from the Town Clerk, the models were covered by a white sheet. One model – quite a nice one judging from a casual glance – was only partially concealed, and when reporters were seen looking in its direction, it was hurriedly covered up.

The Town Clerk's announcement was to the effect that the short list of proposals was now reduced to three, on the recommendation of the Planning Consultant.

Early in January 1961 Miss Barron editorialised yet again on the subject of secrecy:

> Transcending everything in immediate interest and importance, of course, is the Bridge Street Development Scheme, about which the community of Inverness knows nothing, thanks to the unparalleled and unwarranted secrecy in which the Town Council's actions have been surrounded. It is long past time that some authoritative statement was made on this subject, and it is to be hoped that at its first meeting of the New Year on Monday the Council will come out into

the open, and tell the citizens exactly how they are discharging their public trust in this connection. The models of the rival schemes selected for the short leet should be put on view at the earliest moment, and the offers made by the development companies disclosed. After all, no offer will suffer, at this late stage of the proceedings, by exhibition of the models and the disclosure of the amounts of the offers. The fact of the matter is that the public have been kept in the dark for too long, and without a shred of justification.

An inquiry into the Development Plan for Inverness was announced in January 1961, with Mr R. H. McDonald, M.C., Q.C. appointed to conduct the inquiry and report to the Secretary of State for Scotland. It was arranged to start the inquiry on 14 February, but last minute hitches and procedural irregularities meant that it had to be postponed for three months. Bailie Pollitt reported that it was being said in the corridors of St Andrew's House in Edinburgh that it was 'typical of Inverness'. Even Provost Wotherspoon was embarrassed.

On 6 March 1961 things boiled over in acrimony at a Town Council meeting when Bailie Pollitt tried once again to get the Bridge Street schemes discussed in public session. His motion was more personal than previously:

That, in view of the close business association now known to exist between Provost Wotherspoon and the chairman of one of the companies offering for the Bridge Street site, no further action be taken on the present proposals meantime and that the whole question be remitted to the Works and Planning Committees jointly for reconsideration.

The motion was defeated. Provost Wotherspoon decided not to stand again for re-election in the local elections in May, retiring on medical advice. This, said a *Courier* editorial, 'was not unexpected'. Miss Barron nevertheless managed a fulsome tribute to his civic service.

Meanwhile, the Labour Party in Inverness weighed in with its own contributions to the letters column in the *Courier*, without shedding much light on proceedings. They provoked R. R. MacEwan to a response:

How can a party which is supposed to believe in planning for the community justify the inclusion of the new Library and Museum in what is essentially a commercial project? Any new Library and

Museum built now is going to have to provide an important public service for several generations to come. If there are special reasons which justify what should be one of the town's key buildings being built in this way then we should know what they are. In the absence of any special reasons we can only fear that what we are going to get will be based not on any real thought for the community's requirements but on whatever can be spared out of the profit which the developer hopes to make from the rest of the site.

The Inquiry into the Development Plan resumed on 23 May, with 30 objections lodged. Inverness Town Council was represented by Mr Alexander Thomson, Q.C., assisted by Mr A. C. Horsfall, advocate. The *Courier* reported each day's proceedings at great length, at times giving verbatim accounts of the testimony and cross-examination, in which the Burgh Architect, Mr Jack Blackburn, was questioned closely but comes over as truculent, uncooperative and inadequately briefed. He was given a particularly hard time by Mr Robert Reid, Q.C., a former pupil of Inverness Royal Academy, appearing on behalf of Inverness Chamber of Commerce and other objectors. After nine days of hearings the Inquiry was adjourned on 2 June, until 11 September.

On 5 June, Provost Allan Ross had to rule the following motion by Mr J. F. G. Harper incompetent:

> That Inverness Town Council passes a motion of no confidence in itself because of the shocking waste of the public's money during the last fortnight, and that in future it will confine its programme to matters of realistic importance, for example, housing, and before any further development is contemplated, it makes sure that it meets the objectors in a proper and businesslike manner.

Provost Ross said that the motion was void of specification and was an absurdity, and he could not accept it.

In the *Courier* for 14 July 1961, Miss Barron drew the battle lines for the next fight: the development of the north side of Bridge Street. Out of the blue, the Falkirk Development Co., Ltd., acting in association with a London property development company, announced plans to apply for planning permission to redevelop the entire north side of Bridge Street. In an editorial headlined 'What Next?' the *Courier* warned all concerned where this was heading:

For if the Town Council had undertaken the development of the south side of Bridge Street, and had not issued a free-for-all invitation to private developers and profiteers to come in and help themselves, we can be very sure that covetous eyes would not be cast to-day at the north side of Bridge Street and all the properties lying beyond. The financiers and development companies can perhaps be forgiven for imagining, because of the Town Council's actings, that in Inverness there is a cow ready to be milked. Maybe there is on the south side of Bridge Street, but over on the other side they may find that it is not a cow but a bull, and a Highland bull at that, ready to use horns and head should the need arise.

The accompanying news story headlined this as an 'Impudent Attempt to Exploit Inverness' and as 'Southern Profiteers' Threat to Business Community.' It all seemed completely absurd.

On 17 July the Town Council met in a special meeting, once again in private session, to discuss the Bridge Street scheme further. Three councillors walked out in protest, saying they would no longer collude in secret discussions. Two others who had voted in favour of a public session elected to stay for the private session, including the redoubtable Gerald Pollitt, as Convener of the Planning Committee. Miss Barron was apoplectic:

INVERNESS FOR SALE!

Is Inverness for sale to the highest bidder? That is the question the citizens of the Town may well ask themselves when they reflect on the conduct and action of the Town Council in relation to Bridge Street. For, 18 months ago, despite protests by townspeople and local professional and business organisations, the Town Council issued an invitation to development companies and financial corporations to submit offers for the re-development of the whole south side of Bridge Street. The properties on that side of the street – with one notable exception – were compulsorily acquired in order that there would be a widened street and an improved approach to the new bridge to be built over the Ness to replace the Suspension Bridge. It is a striking, indeed lamentable, commentary on the utter incompetence of the Town Council that all the buildings acquired to provide the widened street and improved approach, apart from one or two in the immediate vicinity of the bridge, are still standing to-day. While the Town Council have been dithering during the past 18 months about the offers received from the development companies – as they were still doing last night – the handsome new Ness Bridge has been practically completed, and will be officially opened on September 28th by the Rt. Hon. Thomas Johnston. The Town Council's contribution towards town development in Bridge Street during that year-and-a-half has been the creation of a traffic bottle-neck in Bridge Street. And yet this is the body which is the Planning Authority for the Royal Burgh of Inverness!

After ranting against the 'financial bandits' prevalent throughout the country, and bemoaning the arrival of 'South concerns' with their eye on the north side of Bridge Street, she concludes with an impassioned warning:

Let there be no mistake about it. Those financial and development corporations are not coming to Inverness and serving notices on people because they are concerned in any way with the welfare of the town and its people. They are doing so simply and solely because they see opportunities to make a rich financial harvest at the expense of the town and its business community. If the Town Council do not address themselves to the duty they owe the people of the town, and send speculators of that kind packing, no firm or private individual in the Highland Capital will, as we have said, be safe from assault, and Inverness will, in very truth, be for sale to the highest bidder.

On 26 July, the council met (again in secret session) to interview representatives of the three competing companies involved in the Bridge Street scheme. The *Courier*, anticipating this, warned that 'the Inverness of today may well need development, but it is surely not necessary to destroy it wholesale to build the Inverness of tomorrow.' After the meeting, the *Courier* seemed reconciled to the inevitable:

There was a time, and not so very long ago, when the people of Inverness believed that the town belonged to them. But, with the Town Council putting up an area like the south side of Bridge Street to the highest bidder, and with the tacit invitation by the Council to development corporations to come in and help themselves, the Town may soon belong to financial groups in the Lowlands and England,

and the Inverness of to-day and yesterday, with its history and traditions extending back 2000 years, will be gone for ever.

The immediate cause of this gloomy forecast was that it was finally announced that the successful bidder for the Bridge Street re-development was
the Murrayfield Real Estate Co. Ltd. The unsuccessful companies were the
Falkirk Development Co. Ltd, now seeking planning permission for the north
side of Bridge Street, and Scottish Site Improvements Ltd of Glasgow. The
decision was 'practically unanimous'.

In the final wrangle over whether the meeting should be public or private, there was an outburst of exasperation from two participants:

> Mr Jack Fraser, who voted for a private meeting, protested that it
> was ridiculous for any suggestion to go out from the Council Cham-
> ber that the Council were against the general public of Inverness.
> Anything he had done had been in the best interests of the public.
>
> Treasurer Mackay associated himself with Mr Fraser's remarks,
> declaring that the Council were acting in the best interests of Inver-
> ness, and that the public, when they knew what was being done, would
> realise that it would be very favourable to the Burgh of Inverness.

The *Courier* dismissed these sentiments as 'self-satisfied' and 'smugness'.

At this point the expectation was that a Minute of Agreement with the
successful company would be signed in September with demolitions to begin
immediately thereafter. It was predicted that the whole project could be
completed in 15 to 18 months.

Meanwhile, in a welcome distraction, the *Courier* was able to report
that the new bridge, officially named the Ness Bridge, opened to traffic on
7 August 1961, with the official opening by the former Secretary of State for
Scotland, Tom Johnston, planned for 28 September. The Temporary Bridge
and the temporary footbridge were quickly demolished, the new bridge
resurfaced, and everything made ready for the grand opening. Sadly, Tom
Johnston had to cancel his visit, due to ill health, and the bridge was opened
by Provost Allan Ross.

At long last, somebody wrote in to the *Courier* on 22 August, albeit
anonymously, to support what was proposed for Bridge Street:

> Your continued harangue of the Town Council is becoming too tedi-
> ous. Let the councillors have private discussions. Let them take the

time they need to make up their minds . . . Give the Town Council all the support, help and encouragement you can. The Council needs this more than tirades of abuse.

Finally, we wish your "development companies and financiers" good fortune. If they can give us good modern architecture for ugly dirty blocks and lease back premises to the present businesses they will do Inverness a great service. What was good enough for Queen Mary is not necessarily good enough for us.

On 30 August 1961 the Planning Committee of Inverness Town Council voted 7–2 to recommend that the Town Council grant planning permission in principle for the re-development of the north side of Bridge Street. The full council duly voted, by 13–6, to grant planning permission. It was, said the *Courier*, 'selling our birthright'.

The Inquiry into the Development Plan for Inverness resumed on September eleventh, once again covered in great detail by the *Courier*. It ended on 21 September, having lasted for 19 days in all, having started on 23 May and adjourned on 2 June.

The demolitions on Bridge Street now proceeded apace.

Lower Bridge Street after demolition of south side, 1963.

Steeple and Bridge Street, 1965.

This whole saga was an unedifying spectacle from which Inverness Town Council and its officials emerged with little credit and even less credibility. Despite Miss Barron's suspicions, there is nothing to suggest wrongdoing or corruption in any of their dealings, but plenty to suggest that they were out of their depth and completely inadequate in coping with the complexities they faced. Once momentum developed on the path they had chosen, the outcome was inevitable. It is all depressingly familiar.

The demolitions on Bridge Street were completed in short order early in 1963. By the end of January the buildings on the corner of Castle Wynd were gone, 'and some unusual views of the Castle from Church Street have appeared,' said the *Inverness Courier*. In the middle of February, the de- molishers, Messrs James Campbell and Son, attracted quite a crowd when they used a bulldozer to drag down two large chimney heads, on the south side of Bridge Street – 'spectators and passers-by fled to the shelter of shop doorways to escape the dust.' The Mercat Cross and the Clachnacuddin stone were protected by a wooden enclosure from any possible collateral damage. By early March the demolitions were complete, and it just remained to re- move hundreds of tons of rubble. Invernessians were enjoying the open vistas of the Castle and the enhanced view across the river, and some wondered if the amenity of the town centre would not benefit by preserving these new open spaces. But it was too late for that.

For Mabel Skinner, it was all too much. Writing to the *Courier* on 20 March, she said that one of the reasons she enjoyed returning to Inverness after a visit 'South of the Border' was that it remained very different from the 'ugly built-up areas so common down there.' She bemoaned the fact that the shops she valued so highly were going to be replaced by 'an ugly glasshouse', and for those dependent on the tourist industry she warned that people would not exchange one ugly town for another: 'people don't leave towns destroyed by this "disease" in order to see another just the same.' She bemoaned the loss of Faith, Hope and Charity and the Tartan Warehouse and pleaded for at least the use of local stone in the new frontages.

With the Bridge Street battle lost, newspaper correspondents turned to another muddle, the relocation of the library and museum, and the location of a new home for the police station, while new premises were built at Castle Wynd. Eventually it was decided to move the library temporarily to Farra-line Park – where of course it ended up eventually anyway, once it became clear that there was never going to be enough room in the 'new' building for a modern library and museum. In the end, the council changed their collective mind again and moved the library to a temporary home on a site adjoining the Palace Cinema on Huntly Street.

In another delicious irony, in November 1962 the Inverness Field Club celebrated the 400th anniversary of the visit to the town by Mary, Queen of Scots. The speaker, Dr Jean Dunlop (Mrs R. W. Munro) would go on to have a distinguished career as a writer and historian. She confirmed that Queen Mary did visit Inverness in 1562, arriving in the town on 11 September and leaving on the 15th. She was denied access to the castle by Captain Alexander Gordon, on behalf of the 'treacherous' Earl of Huntly. Local tradition as-serts that she stayed in 'Queen Mary's House', on Bridge Street. Under the circumstances the hope of the Field Club that 'only the constant awareness and enterprise of the Invernessians of today can ensure that, in the current era of destruction and redevelopment, the past is also entitled to its place in the future', has a rather hollow ring.

EASTGATE AND OTHER DEMOLITIONS

*

If the 1960s and 1970s were the decades of Bridge Street and its consequences, the 1980s and 1990s were the decades of Eastgate, leaving us with the townscape we inhabit today. Phase 1 of the Eastgate Centre was opened on 28 February 1983, with Phase 2 completed in 2003. The last remaining industrial area of the town centre was swept away, except for the listed building, part of the Falcon Foundry, which was demolished and re-erected in its present position, backing onto the old Station Hotel. The Falcon Foundry took its

The Falcon Foundry office in its original position, top right.

Top: The Eastgate development.
Bottom: Falcon Square in 2010.

The Inverness Auction Market.

name from its founder, John Falconer. Falcon Square preserves the name, in the public space between the Eastgate Centre and the railway station.

The total cost of Phase One of the Eastgate development was £13 million, of which £11 million was contributed by private developers and £2 million by The Highland Council, for site acquisition, roads and street lighting. The initial car park contained space for 650 vehicles, at a charge of 20p for one hour or £1 for all day parking.

One of the casualties of the Eastgate development was the Inverness Auction Market, which on market days was a teeming mass of animals, farmers and transport vehicles.

Across the road from Falcon Square, at the end of Inglis Street, there used to be a spectacular Rose Window in an old chapel building.

Another major casualty of the Eastgate development was the railway goods yard and the Lochgorm Works, once one of the major employers in Inverness. At one point railway enthusiasts campaigned for the preservation of the railway turntable, but in the end they had to settle for surface markings on a supermarket car park.

A new Aquadome opened at the Bught in 1997, adding to an already impressive collection of leisure facilities in that area. The Glebe Street swimming pool opened in 1936, at which time it was proudly described as 'the most up-to-date swimming baths in Scotland', 100 feet long and 40 feet wide, with Olympic-sized diving boards and traditional changing cubicles along the

Top: Inglis Street Methodist Chapel before development.
Bottom: the Eastgate site looking towards the Crown area, the Albert Hotel on the left, the
Plough on the right.

sides of the pool. Renovations and additions in 1984 included a toddler pool, sauna and jacuzzis, and a new reception area preserving and incorporating the original façade – all now demolished, with long delays and complicated disputes between planners and developers.

Top: the Glebe Street Swimming Pool with Pickford's Depositary to the left, 1979.
Bottom: the White House on Thornbush Road.

There have been sundry other demolitions and losses around Inverness. The White House, on Thornbush Road, was demolished in the 1930s for the widening of India Street. It belonged originally to Mr Forbes, a local solicitor, though by the 1840s was the home of Mr MacLennan, the Secretary of the Fishermens' and Mariners' Society.

Top: MacDougall's Hotel on Church Street.
Bottom: inside MacDougall's Hotel.

MacDougall's Hotel, on Church Street, was demolished in the 1960s. A rare series of interior shots recalls a bygone era.

Top: MacDougall's Hotel, entrance hall.
Bottom: the dining room.

The Music Hall, Union Street.

Further along Church Street, the old Caledonian Hotel was demolished in 1966.

The Music Hall on Union Street was one of the foremost venues in Inverness for a wide range of entertainments and public meetings. Opened in 1865, it could seat 1,300 people. It was renovated after a serious fire in 1898 and went on to host the National Mods in 1903 and 1912. It was sold to the Methodists in 1926 and served as their church until another fire destroyed the building in December 1961. The Methodist Church in Inverness was founded by John Wesley himself, in a small room in Rose Street in 1763. Later, the congregation moved to larger premises on Academy Street and built their first church at the corner of Inglis Street and Hamilton Street, just opposite the front door of today's Marks and Spencer store. When this building was badly damaged by fire in 1923 the Methodists moved into the Music Hall, only to purchase the property in 1926 and convert it for worship. This decision was very controversial at the time – many thought the Town Council should have purchased the building and continued its use as a public venue. After the 1961 fire the Methodists worshipped in the Town Hall and eventually built new premises across the river on Huntly Street, opened in 1965.

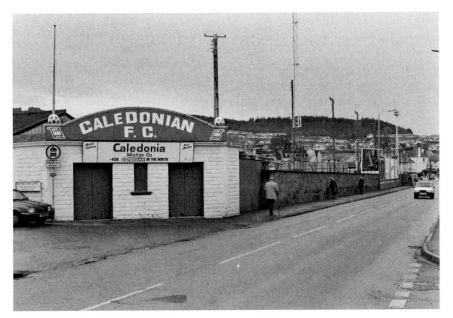

Caley Stadium in 1988.

When the new stadium was built out on the Longman for the new Inverness Caledonian Thistle Football Club, the old Caley Stadium on Telford Street became redundant and was soon demolished to make way for retail outlets. Inverness Caledonian FC and Inverness Thistle FC merged in 1994; Inverness Clachnacuddin FC opted out of the merger. Months of often acrimonious debate and legal proceedings eventually resulted in the longest team name in the Football League. Charles Bannerman bravely attempted to tell the story in *Against All Odds* (1997). Perhaps one day the full story will be told, including the use of public money to clinch the deal for the new stadium. It is difficult to avoid the conclusion that the citizens of Inverness and their public representatives were no more adept at arranging such matters in the 1990s than they had been in the 1960s.

On the western edge of Inverness, above the village of Clachnaharry, overlooking the sea locks of the Caledonian Canal, is the Clachnaharry Monument. This is one structure which was not demolished – it blew down in a gale, in 1934. A fine photograph of 1929 (overleaf) shows it complete, with its statue. This was recovered and taken away 'for safe keeping' by council employees. Needless to say, it has never been seen again. The rest of the structure fell in a storm in the 1950s. The monument was erected in 1821 by Major Hugh Robert Duff of Muirtown to commemorate a clan battle – but almost everything on the explanatory plaque is wrong. It seems that Munros and Mackintoshes were involved, but even the date of this skirmish is debated. The railings which surround the surviving stump are in the form of battle axes.

On the opposite fringes of Inverness, at Culloden, the National Trust for Scotland visitor centre was transformed into an award-winning edifice which opened at the end of 2007.

Top: the Clachnaharry Monument.
Bottom: Culloden Visitor Centre.

Raigmore House, built by Lachlan Mackintosh in the 1820s, was demolished in 1963 and replaced by the present Red Cross House, in the Raigmore housing estate, adjacent to Raigmore Hospital. Before Lachlan Mackintosh returned from India with his fortune this area was known as Broomtown, after the local farm. Lachlan Mackintosh had been born near Tomatin, off

Top: Raigmore House.
Bottom: Northern Meeting Rooms, Church Street.

the A9, south of Inverness, where there were two neighbouring farmsteads, Raigbeg and Raigmore. Raigbeg is still signposted from the main road but its neighbour has disappeared – or rather, migrated to the outskirts of Inverness, where Lachlan named his country estate after his birthplace. Without him, we would be visiting Broomtown Hospital.

Ness House, built in the eighteenth century for Col. John Baillie of Leys, was demolished in 1870 to make way for the Palace Hotel on Ness Walk. After 1854 it was occupied for a while by Royal Engineers on Ordnance Survey work in the Highlands.

Also in 1963, the famous Northern Meeting Rooms on Church Street were demolished, having survived more or less intact since 1790.

Abertarff House, also on Church Street, is one of the very few old buildings to survive – but it used to be hidden from view by other houses. No 69 Church Street and 73-75 Church Street were demolished in 1950, opening up the then quite dilapidated Abertarff House behind.

The town house of the Frasers of Bunchrew was demolished in the 1960s. Dalcross's House, on the corner of Church Street and Queensgate, was demolished in 1900.

By contrast, there is one building in the architectural history of Inverness which was used not for hundreds of years or even for decades, but for only one week! In 1888 the Free Church Assembly was held in Inverness, with

The Frasers of Bunchrew House, Church Street.

148

Dalcross's House, Church Street.

the famous churchman Rev Dr Gustavus Aird as its Moderator. Over 3,000 participants were expected, and in the absence of any suitable accommodation it was decided to erect a temporary wooden building to house them at Ness Walk, where two years later the Palace Hotel was built. John Noble was the joiner in charge – and after being used for only one week his work was completely demolished. This was only the second time the Free Church assembly had been held in Inverness. The first occasion was in August 1845, only two years after the Disruption, when a pavilion for 3300 was erected in Farraline Park, and the classrooms of Dr Bell's School were used as offices.

The *Scottish Highlander* chronicled the demolition of what seems to have been a well-equipped structure:

DEMOLITION OF THE ASSEMBLY HALL

Operations in connection with the removal of the Free Assembly Hall, which has been the scene of so much that is interesting both in the ecclesiastical and the political world, have now been commenced, workmen having been busy during the past two days stripping the inside of the structure and removing the gas and water pipes. We understand that Sir Kenneth Matheson, the proprietor of the ground, was perfectly willing to allow the building to remain for another year, if some arrangement could have been come to whereby this might have been accomplished. Negotiations with this object have failed, however, and many will regret the necessity that has caused an erection so well adapted for the assembly of large bodies of people to be thus removed.

(*Scottish Highlander*, 17 January 1889)

On the west side of the river, some streets (see opposite) have disappeared completely and the townscape is much altered since the nineteenth century. Duff Street consisted of about twenty mainly thatched cottages, running from King Street right through to Wells Street. It was named after the Duffs

Free Church Assembly, 1888.

Top: Green Row, the Maggot.
Bottom: Bisset's Close, Duff Street.

Aerial view of the Royal Northern Infirmary.

of Muirtown, who owned the area as part of their estate. It originally marked the western boundary of the medieval burgh, but has now vanished, apart from a short stretch beside the Thistle Bar. Only the street name survives, at its former junction with Celt Street, to mark the pedestrian entry to the Falconer Court housing development (1980).

In recent years, the sprawling complex of the Royal Northern Infirmary, on the riverbank near Eden Court Theatre, has been reduced to its original core, built between 1799 and 1804. It is now the offices of the University of the Highlands and Islands (UHI).

INVERNESS:
THE DOCUMENTARY RECORD

*

HISTORY BY COMMITTEE

In *The Third Statistical Account of Scotland: The County of Inverness*, edited by Hugh Barron (1985), in the chapter on 'The Parish of Inverness and Bona,' there is an interesting summary of the situation in Inverness at the end of the eighteenth century, after the post-Culloden gloom had abated somewhat:

> In the latter part of the eighteenth century things took on a brighter aspect owing to a more beneficent government policy and also to the undoubted enterprise of the citizens themselves. There was a welcome revival of shipping at the port and considerable rebuilding in the town. In 1791 the Academy was erected and a new court-house and jail took the place of the Old Tolbooth. A Gaelic church was also erected by the heritors of the parish and several other church buildings. A considerable sum was spent on the levelling and paving of streets, several old houses which spoiled the alignment of the main thoroughfare being demolished to facilitate this work.

There was a similar flourishing in the nineteenth century:

> New streets were constructed and the approaches to the burgh widened, and all sorts of social, religious and charitable societies formed. In 1831 the streets were laid with Caithness flags at a cost of £6,000.

It is difficult to know who to credit with these words. The authors of 'The Parish of Inverness and Bona' are listed as:

James Cameron, Esq., former Town Clerk
R. Wallace, Esq., County Clerk
Dr J. A. Maclean, Director of Education
Mr Lawson, Assistant Director of Education

John MacLean, Esq., Harbour Master
George MacBean, Esq., Registrar
Wm. Johnstone, Esq., Director of Social Welfare
Dr Dewar, Assistant Medical Officer of Health
John MacBean, Esq.
Captain Wm. Mackay
and many others too numerous to mention.
Revised and brought up-to-date by
John R. Hill, Esq., Town Clerk
M. Macleod, Esq., Harbour Master
Rev. T. N. Fraser
and others.

History by committee is never a good idea. Their contribution was written in November 1951 and revised in May 1970.

Falcon Square has of course changed drastically since 1970, but the 'Who's Who of Inverness' gives a good description of that area before recent redevelopment:

> Falcon Square is the hub of the wholesale trade in Inverness, and here, or in Dempster Gardens, can be found nearly all the goods the people of the north-east and north, eat, wear or use in the course of their daily lives. The Square, with which are associated the old thoroughfares of First, Second, Third and Fourth Street, carries some alternative names for its highways, Washington Court being an example.

In February 1867, within a matter of a few days, the local newspaper the *Inverness Advertiser* reported the unplanned demise of two old Inverness buildings. First, in the issue of 5 February 1867, a house on Tomnahurich Street:

MELANCHOLY AND FATAL OCCURRENCE

On Friday afternoon, between two and three o'clock, a melancholy accident took place in Tomnahurich Street, by the falling-in of the roof of an old thatched two-storeyed house there. By this occurrence, one man has been suddenly deprived of life, and at least two families have lost their homes, with all they contained. The accident seems to have been caused by the wind having blown the chimney on the roof, and the rafters giving way, the whole mass fell through, the greater portion of the back roof and wall falling with it. The ground floor of the house was occupied by an old man, named Alex. Mackenzie, and his wife. The latter had fortunately just gone out a few minutes previously, but her husband was buried in the *debris*. Upwards of half-an-hour elapsed ere he was got out by a number of men acting under Sergeant Mackintosh, and then it was found that life was extinct. He was very much bruised and injured in various parts of the body, and death must have been almost instantaneous. The body of the deceased was removed to his daughter's house in the neighbourhood of the accident. The upper flat of the house was tenanted by Finlay Maclennan, at one time town crier, and he and his son had a very narrow escape, both being in the room through which the roof and chimney fell. The floor was carried from beneath their feet, and the father managed to make his escape by the window, while the son fell with the rubbish, but singularly he escaped without injury.

At least Mr Maclennan could have made himself heard, if he had had to call for help. This accident took place on Friday 2 February 1867; just three days later, there was another mishap, this time prompting some editorial comment (*Inverness Advertiser*, 8 February 1867):

ANOTHER HOUSE FALLEN IN

We have to record for the second time within the last few days the falling in of an old house, in this instance No. 5, Ness Bank. The domicile was thatched with straw, altogether in a most ricketty condition, and the east end was blown down by the wind about two o'clock on Monday morning. The other end of the house was occupied by Elizabeth Mackintosh, an unmarried woman, who contrived to escape with her life when the timbers were giving way, but who now again occupies the same premises, which to all appearance must soon fall too. The property belongs to Mrs Mackenzie, Dr Grant's Close, and is quite unsafe for human habitation. What are the Guildry Corporation about that human life should be placed at such imminent peril? It is only reasonable to suppose that when two such ricketty buildings are systematically overlooked as those which have been quietly allowed to tumble down within a few days of each other, to the loss of one life and the danger of many more, we may some day or other anticipate a greater calamity through the threatening position of some of the houses in our principal streets – buildings the dangerous state of which is only too conspicuous, and would receive instant condemnation on the conscientious report of any qualified architect. Some explanation of the fatal occurrence of Friday last in Tomnahurich Street might very properly have been looked for at the meeting of Town Council on Monday, but the Dean of Guild was conspicuous by his absence on that occasion.

In these circumstances, it is entirely understandable that when property developers sought to sweep away the rickety remnants of old Inverness, nobody objected; this was Progress.

ARCHITECTS

Almost by definition, architects are more about putting buildings up rather than tearing them down, though sometimes these divergent goals do intersect. In the modern Highlands they are often about sympathetic restoration and there are many examples of excellence in Inverness, most notably Dunbar's Hospital and Abertarff House on Church Street, and Balnain House, the 'Blue House', on the west side of the river. Viewhill House, built by Joseph Mitchell, still stands derelict, after a devastatingly convenient fire. This has prompted differences of opinion in the architectural community – should the façade be restored (the interior was gutted) out of recognition of the importance of Joseph Mitchell in the history of Inverness and the Highlands, or should we admit defeat, demolish the ruins of a building acknowledged to be of no great architectural merit, and make sure that its replacement is worthy of the importance of the site in the townscape of Inverness.

John Gifford, author of *Highlands and Islands* (1992), published by Penguin in the 'Buildings of Scotland' series, had a stab at the beginnings of a history of architects in the Highlands in a paper published in the Annual Report of the Scottish Georgian Society in 1980, entitled 'Architects of the Highlands in the nineteenth century – a sketch'. In it, Gifford acknowledged that 'the architects and architecture of the Highlands have been so little studied that a sketch of the development of architectural practice in the nineteenth century is all that can be offered.' He hoped that his 'rudimentary sketch' would encourage further research, but sadly this remains to be done. Gifford's *Highlands and Islands*, published by Penguin in 1992, collects together in one volume the basic raw material for such a study of surviving buildings, but of course he does not deal with lost and demolished buildings.

Most of the architecture in eighteenth and early nineteenth century Inverness depended on the skills of local tradesmen, coupled with the availability of ornamental detail from suppliers further south. The impetus to establish architectural practices in Inverness came from the east, from Elgin and Aberdeen. William Robertson had settled in Elgin by 1826, in a town renowned for its tradesmen. On his death in 1841 his principal assistant Thomas Mackenzie carried on the practice, entering into a partnership with James Matthews in Aberdeen which continued until Mackenzie's death in 1854. The commission for the head office of the Caledonian Bank in Inverness in 1849 was followed by those for the Free High Church, a lodge at Culloden House and a villa in Inverness.

For the ten years following Mackenzie's death the firm of James Matthews, as it became known, 'was as much an Inverness as an Aberdeen practice,' according to Gifford, with William Lawrie running the Inverness office. They were responsible for such major projects as the Poorhouses in Inverness and Nairn and the Inverness District Asylum. The high point of their achievement was the new Inverness Town House (1878); they were also responsible for the Inverness Markets (1869) and the Royal Clan Tartan Warehouse (1879), along with many churches in Inverness and around the Highlands, and the head offices of the Highland Railway in Inverness. They also did many alterations and extensions of existing buildings.

Thomas Mackenzie's Elgin rivals, A. & W. Reid, established an Inverness office in the 1840s, designing many small houses, farm buildings and churches in and around Inverness and the Black Isle. Smaller architectural practices sprang up in Tain, with Andrew Maitland, and in Inverness with George Rhind, who modestly described himself as a 'builder'. He designed several villas in Inverness, including Lochardil for Charles Fraser-Mackintosh, and several shooting lodges around the Highlands, culminating in Moy Hall and Ardverikie, famous as the location of the TV 'Monarch of the Glen' series.

The most prolific by far of nineteenth-century Highland architects was Alexander Ross – Gifford estimates he was responsible for about 650 buildings. His father James Ross was an architect in Perthshire, moving north in the early 1840s. At his death in 1853 Alexander took over the practice, at the age of only 19, and had designed three churches, two manses and three schools before his 25th birthday. He installed his partner W. C. Joass in a Dingwall office in 1859, 'well placed for picking up numerous commissions in the rich farming area of Easter Ross and the Black Isle,' according to Gifford.

Alexander Ross's two major buildings were the Episcopal Cathedral in Inverness and Duncraig Castle in Lochalsh for Sir Alexander Matheson, both commissioned in 1865. Another major commission was for all the buildings on the north side of Union Street (1863), then being redeveloped, and then almost all the buildings in Ness Walk, Ardross Street and Ardross Terrace, all associated with Matheson and of course controlling the approaches to the Cathedral.

In 1875 Ross's practice designed 65 buildings, including the Bishop's Palace in Inverness and the Inverness Collegiate School, now part of the Highland Council's dreary concrete and glass headquarters on Glenurquhart Road. Gifford describes it as 'built on the scale of a small Oxford college.'

Gifford concludes his paper with a fitting tribute to Alexander Ross:

> Ross was the colossus among Highland architects. Others might be permitted to exist – L. & J. Falconer at Fort William, A. Marshall Mackenzie developing Grantown in the 1870s, John Robertson producing variations on uninspired themes, W. L. Carruthers designing Arts and Crafts villas for Inverness which rank among the best in late nineteenth-century Scotland – but in Ross are drawn together the threads of nineteenth-century Highland architecture, eclectic, practical and at times touching on genius, at others of the drabbest but always stamped with a force of personality which is less often to be found in the recent productions of architects or designers in the Highlands.

Gifford's 1980 paper is extensively referenced, and when taken with his 1992 tome, provides at the very least a starting point for a definitive architectural history of Inverness and the Highlands. It is devoutly to be hoped that one of the doyens of the profession will tackle this admittedly mammoth task.

Reimagining Lost Inverness

One of the joys of living in an historic town is that you can recreate in your imagination events from the past, not in an abstract way, based on research and historical study, but in a shared sense of place, sharing the townscape, the urban space, with friars in the Middle Ages, Jacobites in the eighteenth century – or with your parents or grandparents who in their lifetime have seen Inverness changed; transformed – some would say mutilated – by modern development. Because of the scale of demolitions and redevelopment in the 1960s and 1970s there are still many people in the town who have very immediate memories of living and working in the buildings which are now gone.

Sometimes demolished buildings have more painful and tragic associations. Current Invernessians remember the Glebe Street municipal swimming baths, now demolished. At the time of writing the site is cleared, awaiting development. On 11 May 1911, thirty-four years before the Swimming Pool was built, No 8 Glebe Street was the scene of a particularly tragic crime, now remembered only through the graphic reports in the local newspapers at the time. Isaac Lazarus Silver, a Russian Jew from what is now Latvia, murdered his wife Annie or Hannah in a brutally cruel way – he cut her throat with a razor. He then cut his own throat, while she staggered out into the street and died. A police constable and a doctor arrived within minutes, to find that Lazarus Silver, as he was known, had botched his own suicide; he was patched up, then taken to the Northern Infirmary. When sufficiently recovered, he was tried for murder in Aberdeen, convicted of culpable homicide, because of his mental state, and sentenced to fifteen years penal servitude.

The case attracted lots of publicity, both in Inverness and in the rest of the country. Lazarus Silver was an itinerant pedlar, specialising in jewellery and trinkets. He travelled extensively throughout the northern Highlands and in Orkney – at the time of the 1911 Census, just a month before he murdered his wife, he was lodging at a house in Tain.

His wife was highly thought of by other women in the neighbourhood. Her house was clean, though poorly furnished, and her four children, all girls, were well cared for. Their ages ranged from just under 2 years to 8 years. The eldest child, Mary, was born in Russia the year after the couple were married; she attended Merkinch School. The three others were all born in Inverness, in 1906, 1907 and 1909. It was said that the three oldest children spoke with a perfect Inverness accent.

The family had lived in Inverness for six years, first at 51 Chapel Street (also demolished) and then at 8 Glebe Street. Neighbours spoke about violent rows, and at his trial Lazarus Silver was quoted in evidence as saying that he would have much preferred 'a quiet Scottish lassie' as a wife. Medical evidence suggested quite severe depression and mental illness, with the possibility of brain disease, which was why the murder charge was not pressed too vigorously by the prosecution. The verdict of culpable homicide was recommended by the trial judge and accepted by the jury.

Inevitably, many of the family rows were to do with money. Annie Silver was always short of money and it appears that the final straw was when she sold the family's sofa, one of their few pieces of furniture, to raise the money to move back to Glasgow, where there were friends and family in the local Jewish community, in Govan.

With their mother dead and their father in hospital, and then in prison, the four girls were taken into care, initially in the Inverness Poorhouse. After some months, the baby was sent for adoption to a Jewish family in Dundee, while the three others were boarded out with a crofter in Abriachan for a few weeks, then sent to a Jewish orphanage in London. It is a sad case, made sadder by the fact that no trace remains of either of their family homes. Their only remaining trace in Inverness is Hannah's unmarked grave, in Tomnahurich Cemetery.

The 1911 Census shows that 'The Glebe', the area bounded by Glebe Street, Douglas Row and Chapel Street, to the west of the Old High Church, including Friars' Street, was dominated by overcrowded housing and a largely transient population. Douglas Row is largely intact; Glebe Street has no surviving old buildings; all the residential properties on Chapel Street have gone; only Friars' Street has any nineteenth-century buildings left, though the northern half of that street has been redeveloped with modern housing. This was the area of Inverness where new arrivals could find lodgings, and most of the half a dozen families who made up the small Jewish community lived there.

Inverness Corporation Swimming Baths were opened at Glebe Street in 1936, and modernised and expanded in 1983.

It is tragically ironic that we know quite a lot about what living in No 8 Glebe Street in May 1911 was like, through the newspaper reports of the murder of Annie Silver and the evidence of friends, relatives and neighbours, who often describe daily life in the course of their evidence at the trial. Cases like this are fortunately rare; areas of Inverness which were peaceful and tranquil, escaping the attention of the newspapers, are more difficult to recreate in our imagination.

FIRES

Sometimes buildings were lost and demolished not as the result of planning and progress, but because of accidents, most commonly fire. Sometimes old buildings were the victims of both progress and accidental fire, as in this case in 1868:

FIRE IN CHURCH STREET

On Wednesday night, about eleven o'clock, a fire broke out in an old building immediately adjoining the studio of Mr Fraser, photographer, Church Street. The building, which was recently occupied by Mr Grant, dentist, had been condemned as unsafe, and was in course of being pulled down, simultaneously with the alterations and improvements on the Caledonian Hotel. Workmen had been engaged during the day removing the slates, and it is supposed that the fire must have originated from a spark from some of their pipes falling among the rubbish unobserved. The firemen, who were speedily on the spot after the alarm had been given, soon secured a plentiful supply of water to play upon the premises from a plug on Union Street, and succeeded in extinguishing the fire after the timber of the roof had been burned down, and preventing the flames from spreading to the neighbouring houses. The property belonged to Mr Tait, Church Street, who will be no loser by the fire, as arrangements had just been made for compensation on account of the demolition of the building; but Mr Fraser, the photographer, had considerable damage done to his stock and premises, only a portion of which are insured. (*Inverness Advertiser*, 13 March 1868)

But was this the same property described ten years before in the columns of the same newspaper? Perhaps it was just a coincidence.

Sometimes buildings were lost before they were even completed, as in this example from 1890:

A PARTIALLY BUILT HOUSE DESTROYED BY FIRE

Shortly before seven o'clock on Tuesday evening fire was discovered to have broken out in a house in course of erection at Ballifeary Road for Mr Bell, bookseller, Bridge Street, but before the fire brigade could reach the scene of the outbreak, so quickly did the flames spread, all hope of saving the structure had passed. The Bowling Green, which is in close proximity, being connected by telephone, a number of gentlemen who were enjoying a game immediately communicated with the police office, with the result that the brigade were at once summoned with all possible haste. Mr Macdonald, the fire-master, had meantime, however, been apprised of the occurrence by a gentleman who had observed the smoke from the Castle Hill and securing a cab he was early on the ground taking preliminary measures for dealing with the fire. Nothing, however, could be done to save the structure which by the time the brigade arrived with their apparatus, was completely enveloped in flames, and in about half an hour the whole of the inside of the building had been burnt out, leaving the four bare walls, blackened and cracked as an evidence of the completeness of the destruction. The plasterers and plumbers had been engaged upon the house all day and when they left at six o'clock everything appeared to be as usual. The contract price of the building was between £600 and £700 and the loss, it is understood, is covered by insurance. (*Scottish Highlander*, 19 June 1890)

Sometimes prompt action and lucky circumstances allowed properties to be saved even without the intervention of the fire brigade:

FIRE AT HUNTLY STREET

On Friday morning the Fire Brigade was summoned to the grocery shop, No 47 Huntly Street, where an outbreak of fire was discovered by a baker, who promptly informed the police, a couple of whom rushed to the premises and forced an entrance. They found a chest of tea and the adjacent woodwork in a burning condition. Pails were brought into requisition, and, as the river flows by the opposite side of the road, water was had in abundance. When Mr Macdonald and the members of the Brigade arrived with their hose, the outbreak was extinguished. The damage resulting from the fire was caused mainly by smoke and water. The residents in the adjacent houses, and those staying over the premises, were hurriedly aroused, but fortunately, owing to the prompt [action] taken, they had no serious cause for alarm. (*SH*, 10 July 1890)

In 1890 what we now call the Victorian Market was under development:

THE PUBLIC MARKET

Preparations are now being actively pushed forward for the construction of the new public market. The foundation of part of the structure is now being dug out, and the old Market Inn is being demolished to make way for a new structure more in keeping with the increased traffic of the locality and the handsome markets adjacent. (*SH*, 19 June 1890)

FIRE

Early on Sabbath morning a house in Church Street, adjoining the Caledonian Hotel, was seen to be on fire. The fire originated in a small attic room, some dry wood kept there having been by some accident ignited. Before the fire was observed it had made considerable progress. The alarm having been given, Superintendent Sutherland and the fire brigade were promptly on the ground. Luckily there was a fire plug close at hand, and the hose, which were used without the engines, were worked with capital effect. It was nearly two hours, however, before the flames were got under, and the roof and upper parts of the house have been greatly damaged. Sufficient praise cannot be given to Mr Sutherland for his promptitude and excellent direction of affairs, and to the firemen and policemen under his orders, for their promptness and well sustained exertions throughout the affair. (*IA*, 2 March 1858)

Fortunately, Inverness fires were usually limited in their damage, but in May 1898 there was a major conflagration on Church Street, resulting in significant loss:

ALARMING FIRE IN INVERNESS.

Valuable Property Destroyed.

Intense Excitement.

Last night a great deal of alarm was occasioned in Inverness by an outbreak of fire, the most serious that has occurred in the town for many years. The outbreak took place in that large block of buildings in Church Street, owned by Mr Donald Groat, which has been the subject of recent litigation between the Town Council and the proprietor. The block was an extensive one, of three storeys, having a large frontage to Church Street, and occupied a prominent position in this important thoroughfare. For some time past the greater part has been empty, the only occupant being the proprietor himself who conducts a public-house business in the corner shop on the ground floor. The outbreak, it is believed, occurred in one of the unoccupied rooms on the top flat, and was first discovered about half-past nine in the evening when dense clouds of smoke were seen issuing from the roof. Information was at once conveyed to the Fire Station, and in a very short space of time Fire-master Treasurer and his men were on the scene, and immediately began operations. Three sets of hose were at once connected with adjacent plugs, and these were wrought from coigns of vantage in Baron Taylor's Lane, Church Street, and from the back windows of the corner property on Union Street. At first it was difficult to locate the real seat of the fire, a ruddy glow reflected on the smoke from the back of the ridge of the roof being all that was visible from Church Street. Soon, however, fiery tongues of flame were seen to issue from the roof, and the brigade turned their attention to keeping them within bounds. On the north side, the burning buildings were flanked by large piles of valuable property, in which were the business premises of Messrs Ferguson & Macbean, the well-known firm of jewellers; A. Robertson & Co., tobacconists; Messrs A. Macbean & Sons, tailors and clothiers; A. & D. Macdonald, butchers; A. & S. Fraser, drapers, and many others. The second and third flats were occupied as offices by Messrs C. A. Hendery, architectural surveyor; John Robertson, architect; James Forsyth, solicitor; A. Lauder Hogg, C. E., etc., while the two uppermost storeys were tenanted by Mrs Macdonald, who keeps a private lodging-house, and by Miss Davidson, West End Hotel. It was to prevent the fire doing any damage to these buildings, the gable of which abutted on the burning pile, and thus communicating with Union Street, that the brigade directed their attention in the first instance. Though a copious supply of water was kept pouring on the flames they continued to spread with alarming rapidity and for a time grave fears were entertained of the safety of the adjoining tenements, a number of the occupants beginning to remove the most valuable portion of their belongings. The excitement of the immense crowds which had long ere this gathered round the flaming buildings, blocking up the streets, was intense, and the assistance of an extra force of police which Chief-Constable Macdonald quickly summoned, was required to keep the people in check. After about fifteen minutes' steady application of water, however, a slightly perceptible effect was produced, and the exertions of the firemen were renewed with greater vigour than ever. Then one of the firemen mounted a ladder from Church Street and breaking away the lower sash of the central attic window, the nossle of a hose was inserted, soon taking effect. From this point it was evident that the fire had been got under control, the flames began to decrease, and the excitement of the onlookers, which had reached fever heat, began to abate, numbers shortly after leaving. Water was kept pouring in a regular deluge over the buildings until the flames were subdued and there was no longer much fear of a renewal of the outbreak. As a precautionary measure, however, the firemen kept playing till an early hour this morning on the smoking buildings, the roof of which has been completely destroyed. The entire building has been gutted, and the great quantities of water poured into it has doubtless done irreparable damage to the stock of liquors in Mr Groat's premises. A building at the back of Union Street, used by Messrs A. & S. Fraser, and others as workshops and stores was also completely gutted and the goods, almost wholly of a perishable nature, rendered valueless. It is understood that the bulk of the property is insured.

In the course of the morning, Thomas Macdonald, a young lad who had ventured to the assistance of the firemen was rather severely injured on the back by falling slates. He was conveyed by Sergeant Shaw to the Fire Station, and after a rest was able to go home.

While the excitement was at its height, additional interest was produced on the immense crowds assembled by the report that a second fire had occurred on High Street. Several members of the brigade proceeded to the spot, when it was discovered that an outbreak had taken place in the workshop of Messrs Thomas Kerr & Son, bootmakers. The water was turned on, and in a few minutes the fire was quenched, comparatively little damage being done. It is suspected that by some means the fire had been set going by the gas, the jet having been found burning. (*SH*, 12 May 1898)

Donald Groat had been in the public presses just a few weeks before, when the Town Council took him to court to block his plans to demolish his Church Street properties.

It is interesting to compare coverage of the same events in different newspapers, and the Church Street fire of May 1898 certainly gave newspaper reporters an opportunity to display their descriptive powers. The *Inverness Courier* was more than up to the challenge:

SERIOUS FIRE IN CHURCH STREET

A Block Destroyed

The old block of buildings which forms the junction of Church Street and Baron Taylor's Lane was practically destroyed by fire on Wednesday night. It comprised the three shops and two storeys of dwelling houses over them, numbering from 16 to 20 Church Street. For many years the corner shop was owned and occupied by Mr

John Ross, who disposed of the block a few years ago to Mr Donald Groat. The block was a bit dilapidated, and a long way behind the age, and for those reasons it was without tenants, Mr Groat conducting the licensed business personally. It had been his intention to pull down the building. As it abutted beyond the line of Church Street, the Town Council desired that the new block should be kept within the line. The parties failed to see eye to eye, and a somewhat unfortunate course of litigation ensued, Mr Groat deeming it wise to delay operations on the old building until the dispute was closed. We understand that he had plans and everything ready for the work, and circumstances now necessitate its being proceeded with.

Smoke was seen belching from the roof of the building about half-past nine in the evening. The alarm was raised, and the Fire Brigade, under Mr Treasurer, was on the ground a few minutes after. Water plugs were convenient, and three lines of hose were attached to them and passed up to points on the buildings in the lane, in Church Street, and at the rear of the block in Union Street, which was joined to the burning pile. Great difficulty was experienced in finding the seat of the fire, but it was apparent from the origin of the smoke that it was somewhere near the back of the block. Flames broke through the roof whilst the firemen were at work, and they at once directed their efforts towards circumventing the progress of the fire. The immense crowd of quiet and orderly people who looked on expressed anxiety for the safety of the fine block at the corner of Union Street, as it practically overlooked the flames. The Brigade were perfectly alive to the risk involved, and the supply of water was poured upon the north end of the burning block. Still the flames continued to burst forth, and some of the tenants in the Union Street block removed valuables from their premises. The scene in the street was one of great excitement, but Chief-Constable Macdonald had placed numerous policemen on duty, and nothing untoward was done on the part of the crowd. War was fiercely raging between the elements of fire and water, and, after a time, it looked as if the fire was beginning to give way. Fireman James Macdonald, with some pluck, ascended a ladder which had been placed against the burning pile in Church Street, and he knocked a hole in a window on the third floor. The nozzle of a hose-pipe was thrust into the hole, and the water seemed to fall upon the seat of the fire. At all events, the flames gradually weakened, and the excitement abated. The flood of water was kept flowing on for some hours, whilst the flames sputtered with less and less brightness, and finally all trace of the actual fire disappeared, leaving behind little more than the four walls and a part of the roof of the old block. Internally, the fire must have burned intensely, for the wood work was wholly destroyed. The cause of the fire is unknown, but the evidence goes to show that it started on the ground floor, at the rear of the unoccupied shop at the north end adjoining the Union Street corner. The fire caught the wood staircase, and burned its way to the upper part of the building, doing material damage before the flames burst through the roof. Some stores and workshops at the rear of the building, including one occupied by Mssrs A. & S. Fraser, were also burned down, and the total value of the property and goods destroyed is very considerable. It is understood to be covered by insurance. The Fire Brigade were complimented on the smart manner in which they tackled their work. (*IC*, 13 May 1898)

Taken together, these two accounts give a vivid description of the fire, but also a lot of interesting background information about the occupancy and working life of an old Inverness building. In both accounts it is notable that there is no speculation about how the fire started, and that both accounts mention the planning dispute with the Town Council and the insurance coverage. On balance, the *Scottish Highlander* has perhaps the more gripping description of events, and a more comprehensive list of occupants, while the *Courier* does better in giving the context of Donald Groat's plans and difficulties.

Disappointingly, the *Highland News*, who might even have graced their pages with a photograph of the damaged buildings, were able only to muster a short account, though with perhaps the most explicit linkage between the planning dispute, the fire, and the insurance:

THE CHURCH STREET LITIGATION

Fire Intervenes

Mr Groat's Property destroyed

The large block of houses and shops, which occupied a prominent place at the corner of Baron Taylor's Lane and Church Street, was on the 18th inst. destroyed by fire, and for a time the occupants and proprietors of neighbouring properties were greatly excited lest their goods and chattels should meet a similar fate. As is well known, there has been considerable litigation between **Mr Groat** and the Town Council regarding the question of compensation for removing the building back to the street line, and ultimately the proprietor decided to pull the place down. That has now been accomplished, although somewhat prematurely. About ten o'clock on Wednesday evening it was observed that the place was on fire, and soon after the arrival of the Fire Brigade the flames broke through the roof. For a time the handsome corner property in Union Street was in imminent danger; but by unremitting labours on the part of **Mr Treasurer** and his men, the outbreak was confined to its original quarters, the entire building being gutted. In Mr Groat's spirit shop at the corner of the property a large amount of damage was done to the stock by smoke and water. Most of the property destroyed is covered by insurance.

During the progress of the fire a lad named Thomas Macdonald, who was assisting the firemen, was injured, although fortunately, not seriously, by falling from the roof of a shed. (*HN*, 21 May 1898)

The replacement building, York House, was built by 1900 and survives today.

Sometimes when demolitions were planned, the bureaucratic hurdles to be surmounted are strikingly similar to what we face today:

INTIMATION.

WILLIAM LAURIE, Architect, Inverness, Surveyor of the Commissioners of the Burgh of Inverness, appointed under the Police and General Improvements (Scotland) Act 1862, has presented a **PETITION** to the Sheriff of the County of Inverness, setting forth that the **PREMISES, No 31 HUNTLY STREET, INVERNESS,** are in a **RUINOUS STATE**, and **DANGEROUS** to **PASSENGERS** and to the Occupiers of the neighbouring Buildings; that the Owners of said Premises are not known, and not resident within the Burgh of Inverness; and that he had caused a Notice to be put up on the most patent door of the said Premises, requiring the Proprietors thereof to take down the same, and intimating that, failing their beginning within Three Days after said Notice to take down said Premises, and completing the taking down thereof as speedily thereafter as the nature of the case would admit, he would make complaint thereof to the Sheriff – all in terms of the 236th section of the said Act; and setting forth, further, that the said space of Three Days had elapsed, and that the Proprietors of said Premises had failed to begin to take down the same; and praying the said Sheriff, upon such inquiry as his Lordship might deem requisite, to order the Proprietors of said Premises to take down the same, or such part thereof as should appear to be in a dangerous state, within such short time as might be fixed by his Lordship. Upon considering which Petition, the Sheriff-Substitute of this date pronounced an Interlocutor, remitting to Mr William Reid, architect, Inverness, and Mr John Ellis, builder, Inverness, to examine and report whether the said Premises are in the state alleged in the Petition; and appointing notice to be given of the presentation of said Petition once in each of the *Inverness Courier* and *Inverness Advertiser* newspapers; and ordaining all parties interested to appear within the Sheriff's Chambers, Inverness, personally or by an agent, on Monday, the twentieth instant, at Ten o'clock forenoon, if they intend to oppose the prayer of the Petition.

Of all which intimation is accordingly hereby given.

JO. MACLENNAN, Agent for the Petitioner, Inverness, sixteenth July 1868

(*IA*, 17 July 1868)

One of the earliest planned demolitions took place in 1852, in connection with building the new bridge over the Ness, replacing the one swept away in the 1849 floods. Here the *Inverness Advertiser* bemoans the march of Progress:

THE NEW BRIDGE

Active operations as regards the erection of the new bridge have now been begun, although the commencement is in the way of demolition. Sacrilegious hands have been laid on Castle Tolmie; and, by the exertions of Mr Henry's workmen, that venerable and substantial fabric, which has withstood the blasts of some two hundred years, will speedily be levelled with the ground. It was a sturdy pile of building, and might well shame the slim and hastily run up workmanship of these degenerate days. It is proposed to go on with the formation of the coffer-dams immediately after, and to advance the works with all celerity. We trust the plans now put forward may be acted on, and that the anticipations of success which are entertained may be realized. (*IA* 2 March 1852)

Just three years later, the work was nearing its conclusion:

THE NEW BRIDGE

Yesterday morning the demolition of the foot-path bridge which has served as a means of communication with the west side of the river since the flood of 1849, was commenced, its removal being necessary to the completion of the mason work for the new structure, which is now so far advanced that foot passengers will suffer no inconvenience. The work seems as if the bridge would admit of being opened ere the wool-market. And it is time, surely, that this would happen! From an advertisement in another column it will be seen that its cost has far exceeded the estimate. That was £15,400 for the bridge, and £3000 for the approaches. An excess of expenditure to the amount of £6000 is now reported; and probably that may not cover the whole deficiency, for those entitled to compensation will now be much more difficult to deal with than if the works had been finished within the time first stipulated. By the way, the question occurs very naturally, what is to become of the materials of the old foot-path bridge? (*IA*, 26 June 1855)

As the bridge neared completion, the townsfolk of Inverness became increasingly impatient with the slow progress. The Wool Market came and went, and still it was not finished. A public meeting was held to allow citizens to vent their feelings, and in the middle of August the workmen, fed up with public criticism, pinned a copy of the *Courier* to their workplace, with the coverage of the public meeting outlined by a black border of pitch. The *Inverness Advertiser* thought they had gone too far: 'This was a piece of bravado, to the full as silly as it was impudent.' (*IA*, 14 August 1852) However, by 28 August they had good news to report:

THE NEW BRIDGE

The New Bridge has at last been finished. Passengers are now allowed to cross and recross daily. We know not if any civic ceremonial is intended to be held in celebration of the event. Upon the principle that "good gear should be welcomed," there ought to be some public demonstration.

Occasionally 'Improvements' were welcomed, though sometimes little evidence survives today:

IMPROVEMENT OF THE CASTLE HILL

It affords us much gratification to learn that the Castle Commissioners, at a meeting held by them on Friday, resolved to take the requisite preliminary steps for carrying out a much-needed improvement on the Castle grounds. The present bare and unsightly aspect of the hill renders it a grievous eyesore to every one gifted with the slightest modicum of good taste as regards the picturesque; especially when its capabilities of embellishment are taken into consideration. We understand that a plan for its improvement, drawn out by our townsman, Mr G. G. Mackay, was submitted to the meeting. This sketch we have seen. It seems to us very tasteful in itself, and admirably adapted to the situation. According to it, the whole extent would be suitably laid off in walks and parterres, and be rendered a piece of "verdant sculpture", such as would adorn the appearance of the dignified pile of building, and impart an invigorating freshness to its "pleasant seat." It is proposed to erect a *jet d'eau* or a statue in the centre, and to enclose the whole, having a gate at the extremity towards the Haugh road, and another with a porter's lodge on the side facing View Place. We trust that Mr Mackay's plan, although its adoption may entail some expense, will ultimately be sanctioned in all its fullness by the Commissioners, and perhaps its carrying out may be made a gradual process. (*IA*, 2 March 1852)

There are a few cases where the only surviving image of a building has to be conjured indirectly. One such is the Culloden Brick and Tile Works, long gone, but in this newspaper notice something of its former glory can be retrieved:

CULLODEN BRICK & TILE WORKS

The Subscriber, formerly of the firm of McNab & Campbell, in returning thanks to Customers and the Public generally for the very liberal patronage bestowed on them, begs to intimate that he is now Sole Lessee of the **CULLODEN TILEWORKS**. They are the most extensive Tileworks known, while the Machinery is constructed on the most approved principles, both for speedily executing and producing a superior article, being capable in the eight working months of making from three to four millions of Machine-made Drain Tiles and Pipes. These are, of course, exclusive of a vast number of Bricks and hand-made Tiles constantly in process of manufacture.

To prevent disappointment to parties ordering in the Pottery line, which often occurred when the portion of the premises allotted to that branch was more limited, and the hands employed were fewer, ample room is now provided for the accommodation of as many men as will meet any probable demand, while that branch is to be under the direction of one of the best Water-Pipe makers of the day. In connection with Glazed Close-jointed Pipes, Flower-Pots, &c., it is intended to manufacture Brownware, principally for Dairy purposes, as Milk-Plates, Butter-Jars, &c.&c., some of which will be ready for sale in course of a few weeks.

There is now on hand a quantity of common Drain Tiles and Pipes, common and Circle Bricks, Glazed and Unglazed Close-jointed Water-Pipes, Chimney-Cans, Flower-Pots, &c., of all sorts; Welsh Slates, for drain soles; all of which will be delivered at any port or beach as formerly. Also on hand at the Culloden Tilework Store, Petty Street, Inverness, a supply of Fire-clay Vases, with Pedestals to match; Chimney-Cans, of all patterns, from 2 to 6 feet high; Fire-Bricks, and Fire-Clay.

Customers and all who may transmit their commands are assured that they will be supplied with the very best articles with the utmost possible despatch; while it is requested that all orders be given in writing, and as long previous to the commodities being actually needed as possible, in order to prevent disappointment. Further particulars will be given in future advertisements. All communications to be addressed to the Subscriber, who alone is responsible for all transactions done on account of the concern on and after the 4th inst.

DANIEL CAMPBELL
Culloden Tile Works,
Inverness, 4th February 1852.
(*IA*, 2 March 1852)

THE OLD TOWN HALL

THE OLD TOWN HALL

The work of pulling down the buildings on the site on which the new Town Hall will rise was commenced on Monday morning. The first act was the removal by the iron-work contractor – Mr William Smith, son – of the gas lamp in front of the old Town Hall, and immediately above the venerable Clachnacuddin stone. Thereafter, the demolition of the Commercial Hotel adjoining the present hall was commenced by the carpenter contractor – Mr D. Macpherson. The Town Council will meet once more yet in the old Town Hall – on Monday first. It has been arranged that everything of interest connected with the present building shall be carefully preserved. It is proposed that the "Clach" stone shall be placed at the edge of the Exchange on the spot where the water fountain now stands. In the windows of the hotel in Castle Wynd, and in various parts of the Town Hall, there are carved and inscribed panels and pediments, which are also to be preserved. By the courtesy of the Commissioners of Supply, the Council will meet, while the new hall is being erected, in the Convening Room of the Castle. (*IA*, 3 May 1878)

To this the *Inverness Courier* added:

The demolition of the Commercial Hotel adjoining the present hall was commenced by the carpenter contractor – Mr D. Macpherson – who by yesterday had removed all the doors, windows, and wooden partitions in the building, which now presents to High Street and Church Street a woeful spectacle indeed.

The Council duly met on 6 May and had a 'pleasant meeting', during which the Provost and others made speeches about how much they would miss the old building, and duly toasted it with a glass of wine. Bailie Black read a brief extract from Macaulay's 1689 description of Inverness:

The Exchange was in the middle of a *miry street* in which stood a market-cross much resembling a broken mile-stone; though the sitting of the Municipal Council were held in a filthy den with a roughcast wall; though the best houses were such as would now be called hovels; though the best roofs were of thatch; though the best ceilings were of bare rafters; though the best windows were in bad weather closed with shutters for want of glass; though the humbler dwellings were heaps of turf in which barrels with bottoms knocked out served the purpose of chimneys; yet to the mountaineer of the Grampians this city was as Babylon or as Tyre. Nowhere else had he seen 400 or 500 homes, 3 churches, 12 malt kilns crowded together; nowhere else had he been dazzled by the splendour of rows of booths where knives, horn spoons, tin kettles, and gaudy ribands were exposed to sale.

Not just Councillors attended this meeting; there was a good representation of ministers, lawyers and other worthies. One of the guests was James Fraser, a former Town Councillor and possibly the oldest inhabitant of Inverness. Before concluding, they managed another toast, another glass of wine, this time toasting the health of the Provost.

Councillor Matthew Elliot, described by the *Inverness Advertiser* as 'one of the teetotal fraternity who is gifted with a singular propensity in certain public matters of, to use a common phrase, "putting his foot in it," ' rather spoiled the occasion by objecting to the dispensing of wine.

Rather sweetly, in pulling down the mantelpiece of the Commercial Hotel one of the workmen found a love letter, dated 19 November 1815, written by a woman from the Portree Wool Mill. The writer of the letter, said the *Advertiser*, was 'not particularly well educated' but the letter 'abounds in endearing expressions.'

As is often the case in these matters, some locals decided to dissent publicly from the latest manifestation of Progress:

ASSOCIATION FOR THE PRESERVATION OF THE EXCHANGE, INVERNESS

The members of this Association view with feelings of deep regret the proposal of the Town Council to build over the ancient Exchange, which, as the centre of the town, and the site of the Clachnacuddin stone, is invested with associations of much interest.

The buildings of any architectural pretensions possessed by Inverness, apart from the Castle and ecclesiastical edifices, surround the Exchange – viz, the ancient spire, which is a model of elegant proportion, the Caledonian Bank, the Christian Association Buildings, and when the new hall is built, the Hall itself. Space is absolutely essential to the dignity and exhibition of architecture. It is now a received axiom that, without suitable space, money and skill expended in architecture are simply thrown away. Notable examples of how fine buildings are lost in narrow streets are to be seen in Glasgow, where handsome structures are passed without their existence being observed.

In modern cities the first requisite in founding a public building is to secure space where it may be properly seen and its beauty appreciated. And in most places where any great buildings of old date exist, the houses which formerly were crowded around them have been or are being pulled down to give light and space. The Inverness Town Council is doing the opposite. It is putting up a new and costly building of architectural pretensions, and at same time encroaching to a destructive extent on the already too narrow space in which it is to be set, and it is also marring in a manner deeply to be deplored the effect of the other fine buildings abutting on the square.

Nothing but overpowering necessity could excuse or palliate such an act of vandalism, and this Association is formed for the purpose of protesting against it, and if need be, of taking such measures of prevention as may be thought expedient.

The following are some of the names of townsmen appended to the foregoing, which has been forwarded to us for publication: Mr Waterston, banker; Mr Macandrew, sheriff-clerk; Mr Colvin, solicitor; Mr Rule, banker; Mr J. H. Mackenzie, bookseller; Mr John Chisholm, ironmonger; Mr James Ross, solicitor; Mr Jonathan Ross, merchant; Mr R. H. Grant, solicitor; Mr Allan Macdonald, solicitor; Mr R. Naughton, jeweller; Mr J. Fraser, chemist; Mr J. G. Campbell, solicitor; Mr W. Ferguson, jeweller; Mr Duncan Cameron, merchant, Union Street, Mssrs Rose & Cameron, bonded stores; Mr T. G. Henderson, wine merchant; Mr Robert Grant, Tartan Warehouse; Mr W. M. Snowie; Mr W. Mackay, solicitor; Mr Campbell, draper; Mr Reid, architect; Mr Alexander Ross, architect; Mr Rhind, architect. (*IA*, 24 May 1878)

This was certainly an impressive assemblage of professional and commercial talent, and their 'manifesto' is interesting as it clearly incorporates principles of architectural design which would be readily familiar to practitioners today. However, the *Inverness Advertiser* was not impressed: 'We are at a loss to understand the sudden anxiety betrayed by an undoubtedly influential section of the community.' They pointed out that the proposals had been published and discussed three months before, and adopted by the Town Council. Resisting the temptation to suggest architectural and legal sour grapes, they conceded, just, that their motives were 'a sincere desire for the best interests of the community.'

Warming to his theme, the editor of the *Advertiser* took flight:

We hear of the architectural effect of the Town Hall being marred and the surrounding buildings dwarfed; but that is a matter of opinion, our own notion being that the buildings will be shown to quite as much advantage as their merits deserve. As for revered associations connected with the place, the recollection of street preachers, teetotal lecturers, and the barter of butter, eggs, and poultry is scarcely hallowed to the memory; and the "Clach" and the cross can be suitably placed in connection with this new building. We hold that it is unwise and impolitic to re-open the matter at this stage – to hint at throwing a burden on the ratepayers by the acquisition of more property in the vicinity, and to run the risk of law suits with the contractors for breach of contract. Those townsmen who suggest that the open space referred to does not belong to the town, and accuse the guardians of the public interest of appropriating what is not their own – who threaten to interdict the Council in the prosecution of an undoubted public improvement – should moderate their opposition somewhat until the mind of the community is ascertained on the subject. Meanwhile they should remember that by three months silence they are understood to have already given their consent to what they are now declaring to be a public grievance. (*IA*, 31 May 1878)

All this precipitated a lively but ultimately futile correspondence in the local papers. The Editor of the *Inverness Courier* added his own thoughts:

THE EXCHANGE

Our readers are aware that a movement is on foot to prevent the encroachment of the new Town Hall on the Exchange. An association has been formed, and a deputation is to meet the Council on Saturday. The public should clearly understand that this is not a question affecting architects, but solely a question affecting the appearance and amenity of the town. The movement is perhaps a little late, as the contracts for the new building have been signed, and the old hall demolished, but if it is still practicable to retain the full depth of the Exchange, we cannot understand how any person could venture to question the propriety of its preservation. Most communities are anxious to have as many open spaces as possible; but in this case it is proposed to cut off a large portion of the only public Place or Square we possess - to narrow the thoroughfare, destroy the old familiar aspect of High Street, and mar the artistic effect of the new hall and all the surrounding buildings. In reply to the complaint of delay, it may be stated that to this hour the plans have not been exhibited, nor has any official statement been made as to the full extent of the contemplated encroachment. It seems now to be generally understood that the buildings are to be carried forward seven feet on the side of Castle Street, and some distance variously stated to be from sixteen to twenty-six feet on the side of the Castle Wynd. Such a change as this obviously calls for more careful consideration than it has yet received, for, if the public are rightly informed on the subject, the effect would be to reduce the whole street to the character of an almost unbroken line. The front of the Town Hall would no longer be the central rallying point of Invernessians on occasions of popular interest: and it would cease to be, as it has been hitherto, the Forum of Inverness. (*IC*, 6 June 1878)

The *Courier* returned to this theme a week later:

That the encroachment is a mistake appears to be generally acknowledged. One of the peculiarities common to old towns – where innovations have not destroyed original features – is that such spaces are preserved in front, or directly in connection with, municipal buildings. This is the case, almost without exception, in the old towns of France, Germany, and the Netherlands, the spot being regarded as a public place for the inhabitants to resort to on occasions of public importance. Inverness is a small town at best, and if a lofty building is allowed to advance beyond the bounds of the present hall, no one can estimate, before it is put up, how much the appearance of the centre of the town may be prejudicially affected. The members of Council must be sensible of this, and we believe they will do their best to prevent the mischief. (*IC*, 13 June 1878)

Now of course, Invernessians have Falcon Square as a public space, though it is located not in front of an important municipal building but is adjacent to that temple of commerce, the Eastgate Centre.

The controversy took on a rather unpleasant personal tone when a letter in the *Inverness Advertiser* appeared to impute suspect motives to the architectural community. Local architect John Rhind was not slow to respond, in the pages of the *Inverness Courier*, and as his letter is quite revealing as to architectural standards and practice at the time, it is worth quoting:

THE EXCHANGE ENCROACHMENT

Sir, – In a letter which appeared in the *Advertiser* of Tuesday, "One of the Community" clearly points to one of the architects as being the cause of the present agitation about the new Town Hall, and as I have done more in this matter than perhaps any of the others, I think it is possible that I am the architect referred to.

Allow me to state that from the beginning, both as an architect and as a citizen, I had no other wish than that the town should have the benefit of the best design (whoever the author might be), consistent with honour and justice; but I must confess that I do not and cannot yet understand on what principle it is that the set of plans which grossly violates almost all the instructions given by the Council should be that adopted. For some time I certainly did think that the successful competitor must have had received different instructions from the others in the competition; but the Provost, at a recent meeting of Council, settled this question by a flat denial, leaving us with the only other alternative, viz., that the said author has presumed to encroach, as he did on the Exchange Square, on his own responsibility, which encroachment, if not formally allowed beforehand, was certainly afterwards sanctioned by the Council. I leave the intelligent public to say whether this was not a matter of injustice to the other competitors whose designs could have been built within the prescribed limit indicated by the block plan accompanying the Council's instructions.

And all we are now told by the Council is that we are too late to object at this stage. But, I ask, why did not the Council look into this matter before they had advertised for contracts? For even before then they had received my letter, in which I drew their attention to the whole subject, and in which I also warned them as to serious consequences. That letter is still on their table, and, so far as I know, without receiving the slightest consideration. And, I am sorry to say, they had not the common courtesy to reply to it – a treatment which I am not accustomed to receive when I communicate with gentlemen, and which I certainly did not expect especially from the very gentlemen who have put me to the trouble and expense of preparing elaborate plans, and from which, as I shall hereafter prove, they have largely benefited.

JOHN RHIND

(*IC*, 13 June 1878)

If all this has echoes of the great Bridge Street fiasco in the 1960s, it just goes to show that there is an apparently inevitable tendency for bureaucracies not to learn from history.

The detail of the ensuing debate is tedious, but one anonymous scribe, signing himself 'Andreanus', has a particularly prescient passage:

The proposed encroachment is peculiarly inappropriate in this town of all others. Inverness is nothing if not beautiful. In default of manufactures it must rely on its social and aesthetic attractions. It is, in fact, a reproduction on a smaller scale of Edinburgh. There the authorities are ever watchful to preserve and increase its amenity; and the same policy must be pursued here if the town is to maintain its prestige as the Highland Capital. (*IC*, 20 June 1878)

The situation was resolved when the Council purchased the property immediately to the rear of the Town Hall site, allowing a public space in front to remain. Legal proceedings were averted and the project was back on track, much to the relief, no doubt, of the successful architects, Alexander Ross and his partner, William Lawrie.

Often demolitions warranted just a tiny paragraph in the local papers, even when they would seem to us worthy of further comment, as in this case from 1858:

THE CITADEL BUILDINGS

The demolition of the Citadel buildings commenced early in last week, and is now well advanced. The buildings were old and out of repair, but were of considerable strength, and might have been turned to account for many years to come. (*IA*, 16 February 1858)

The idea that buildings have a finite working life and should be replaced when they have served out their time is built into architectural design today, but we often have trouble applying that principle to historic buildings, whose value to society sometimes now exceeds their practical use.

Occasionally the papers were prepared to pause and reflect on the previous history of a building, as in this example in 1867:

REMOVAL OF AN OLD HOUSE IN BRIDGE STREET

The subjects in Bridge Street, lately purchased by Mr D. Mackenzie, grocer, having been condemned by the Guild Court, have been taken down, and will shortly be rebuilt. Some notice of the former possessors might not be uninteresting.

Prior to the year 1651, the property belonged to William Paterson, a member of that once influential burgher family, who not only held a great deal of town land, but also the estates of Inshes and Bught. In November 1651, Paterson disposed to Gregor Grant of Gartallie, in Glen Urquhart, who carried on business in Inverness, and possessed several acres of land at the Lochgorm. Gregor Grant fell into embarrassed circumstances, but having been assisted by Colonel Patrick Grant, Tutor of Grant, and one Donald vic-Homas-Roy in Redcastle, struggled on, leaving the Bridge Street property to his son James Grant, described as "Chapman in Inverness," who was infeft, 24th October 1699. This James, who married Lillian Hossack, was succeeded by a son named James, who died without issue in 1714. Upon 18th August 1716, Alexander Grant of Sheuglie, whose unhappy fate is well known, was served heir to this last James Grant, the propinquity being really Highland cousinhood, for he had to go back to "James Grant in Urquhart," the father of Gregor of Gartallie, before he came to the common ancestor. Sheuglie sold the property in 1718 to Roderick Williamson, periwig-maker in Inverness. This was at one time an important trade, and was sometimes combined with that of doctor or apothecary. At the beginning of last century, John Macrae, "chirugeon and periwig maker," was a person of note in Inverness. In 1727, Williamson sold the house to Donald Mackenzie or Kilcoy, who was succeeded by his son Colin. Colin of Kilcoy disposed to Hugh Inglis, shipmaster in Inverness, in the year 1743. Captain Inglis's immediate neighbour was also a shipmaster, Donald Mackintosh, father of the celebrated merchant known as "Skelpan Sandy." Both Captains Inglis and Mackintosh were capital men of business, as we judge from their letters, many of which belonged to us. They sailed their own crafts, always armed, generally to London. But not unfrequently to French and Dutch ports, just as Great Britain might happen to be at peace with these

Powers. Had space permitted, we would gladly have given two of Captain Donald's letters, one intimating his marriage with Miss Mackintosh, sister of Provost John, afterwards of Aberarder; the other narrating his chase by a French privateer, which he avoided by so closely hugging the Norfolk coast as to deter the pursuit. Captain Inglis was married no less than four times, having, we believe, a family by each wife. His eldest surviving son was Provost William Inglis of Kingsmills, who did so much for the improvement of the town, &c. The property remained with the Inglis family until 1803, when it was sold by George Inglis of Kingsmills to Charles Jamieson, silversmith in Inverness, a most worthy man and honest tradesman. There is no mistake about the silver which bears his mark. Of the few now in Inverness of the old burgh families, nearly all have some of his plate, and if well taken care of, it is "as good as new." The subjects remain with Bailie Jamieson's heirs until sold a few years ago to Mr Mackenzie. (*IA*, 26 March 1867)

There is enough material in this account of the history of just one Inverness building to inspire a novel! Embedded in the very fabric of the building, soon to become a pile of rubble, is a family saga which tells us a great deal about how Highland society worked, with all its linkages and connections. There is so much social history contained in that report; it gives just a little indication of how much is lost when an historic building is demolished: not just the stones, but the stories they contained.

Another example of recognition that a way of life was being demolished along with the buildings can be seen in August 1934 when the Glebe Street site was being cleared in advance of the new swimming pool:

AN INVERNESS LANDMARK
The Site for the New Public Baths

During the past few years several old buildings in Inverness have been demolished to make way for improvements of various kinds, the latest landmark to disappear being the range of tenement houses known as Albert Place. These dwellings have been removed so as to be used as a site for the up-to-date baths to be erected by the Corporation, plans of which were passed by the Dean of Guild Court.

The buildings which have been demolished have quite an interesting history. They were erected 150 years ago for the purpose of carrying on a white and coloured linen and worsted thread

manufactory established in 1783, the proprietors being a company
of local gentlemen who sought to provide employment in Inverness
and other parts of the Highlands. It was a very extensive concern,
absorbing the bulk of the flax grown locally, as well as large quantities imported from Russia and Holland. The thread produced was
sold mainly in the London market, the amount realised from this
source being on an average £20,000 per annum.

The various processes of manufacture, such as heckling, opening, twisting, and dyeing afforded employment to about 10,000
people, young and old. Dr Robertson, in his "Agriculture in the
County of Inverness," published in 1808, says – "This manufactory
is of immense benefit to the country, no fewer than 6000 women are
employed in spinning thread in the different counties of Inverness,
Moray, Ross, Nairn, Sutherland, etc., under the direction of nine-
teen agents in different quarters, who give out the flax, receive the
yarn, and pay the wages."

About 100 men and 150 boys and girls were employed in the
factory here. Men earned from 5s to 10s weekly, and women and children from 2s to 4s. For a short period the thread factory prospered,
but southern competition interfered, and after existing for 30 years
was discontinued in 1813. Some time afterwards the substantially
built premises were converted into dwelling-houses, which came to
be known as Albert Place. (*IC*, 10 August 1934)

One wonders if anybody even considered, back in 1934, that these buildings could have been used to interpret and celebrate an important part of the
industrial and social history of the Highlands. Too late now, with the up-to-
date baths demolished and the site currently lying empty and derelict.

In July 1934 the Town Council met and decided to widen Castle Street
by ten feet; this of course necessitated some further demolitions, following on
from the damage caused by the landslips on the Castle Hill two years before.

On 18 February 1930 the *Inverness Courier* reported on proposed demolitions in the town:

INSANITARY HOUSES

Demolition Orders Passed by Town Council

At a special meeting of Inverness Town Council, held last night –
Bailie William Michie presiding in the absence of Provost MacEwan
– it was agreed to pass orders for the demolition of a number of

dwellings in the town. It was stated that Closing Orders had been obtained in respect of the properties on account of their being considered unfit for human habitation. In some cases it was agreed to suspend the operation of the demolition orders for six months in order that the owners might have an opportunity of effecting repairs. The houses on which the demolition orders were passed were: –

53 and 55 King Street
14 Lower Kessock Street
27 and 28 Shore Street
7 and 9 Lower Kessock Street
86 Castle Street (back portion only)
7, 9 and 11 Pumpgate Street
12 Mid Street, Clachnaharry
3 Chapel Street
68 Chapel Street
48 Grant Street
44 Eastgate
2 Bank Street
4 Pumpgate Street
3 and 5 Lower Kessock Street
12 Lower Kessock Street
74 Huntly Street
49 King Street
51 King Street
1 and 1a Stephen Street
10–12 Market Brae
6 Anderson Square
7 Anderson Square
18 Grant Street
4 Friar's Street
1 to 4 Friar's Court
6 Friar's Street
3 Fraser Street, Haugh
(*IC*, 18 February 1930)

Occasionally letters appear in the public press asking for the beauties of Inverness to be preserved. Often the writers are not residents, but visitors, or in this case (in 1934) somebody who has returned to the town after a long absence:

AN INVERNESSIAN'S COMPLAINTS

Sir, – After an absence of 34 years I would like to make a few re-marks, not in criticism so much as out of love for the town, and hope for its conservation and betterment.

Firstly, may heaven forgive those who were responsible for the erection of that ghastly gasometer and the abominable chimney stalk at the Royal Northern Infirmary. These two hideous erections mar the view of the town, approach it by what route you will.

I would also mention the spoliation of the beautiful Islands by the erection of jazz band enclosures and tawdry arc lights. Surely the most beautiful public park in Europe might have been con-served. I would also request those responsible to clean the town of wastepaper and litter before the arrival of the mass of visitors in the summer and autumn.

I was distressed to see the condition of the gateway entrance to the Castle. Who has taken away the steel gates which so magnifi-cently adorned the entrance that now seems to be so neglected? I saw the excellent improvements that have taken place consequent upon the razing of the retaining wall some two years ago. It aston-ished me, however, to see that no steps were laid from Castle Street to the Castle Hill. It seems a wonderful opportunity wasted.

In conclusion, I would like to refer to the neglect in the case of the Islands. Formerly the banks used to be neatly cut at the edges bordering on the pathways, but now the grass seems to be allowed to grow any way.

Inverness has the reputation of being one of the most beauti-ful and cleanest towns in the country. Let those responsible for its conservation keep it so. – Yours etc.

A RETURNED RESIDENT

(*IC*, 6 July 1934)

Architecture certainly provokes the emotions, so it is no surprise to find words like 'ghastly', 'abominable' and 'tawdry' recurring in public debate. And of course litter is an ongoing problem everywhere.

It is a feature of local newspaper coverage that references to demolitions are either buried in the minutiae of Town Council meetings or are occasioned by some chance discovery made during the work involved. One such instance took place in 1934, when workmen discovered a diary, and some other arti-cles, during the demolition of some buildings in Shore Street:

INTERESTING FINDS IN INVERNESS

Old Diary Discovered in Shore District

When demolishing some buildings off Shore Street, Inverness, the workmen made some very interesting discoveries, which throw some light on the state of that district last century. They discovered what is supposed to be part of a mansion-house over two centuries old. The pannelling and cornice work are still in remarkably good condition. There is a stone built into the wall with a carved face on it. Among the interesting relics found are a receipt form dated 1800; a diary, the entries in which commence on 4th January 1830; some old newspapers; and an Enfield rifle dated 1868, still in good condition.

The receipt form was written in July of the year 1800, and the goods mentioned thereon were purchased from "W. Tait," who is described on the form as a "Hair Dresser, Perfumer, Peruke maker, and Toy man." (*IC*, 17 July 1934)

This report goes on to describe some diary entries in detail, pointing out how it sheds light on business methods, transportation and medical practices at the time. In these more enlightened days we would hope that such chance discoveries would find their way into the safe keeping of Highland Archives, in their new home at the Bught. Of course, in the summer of 1934, both the Editor of the *Courier* and his readers were far more interested in the comings and goings of Nessie: the adjoining column is headed 'Are there two Loch Ness Monsters? Inverness Party's Thrilling Experience.'

Occasionally something of historical importance would turn up in the course of a demolition, as in this example from 1859:

ANCIENT RELIC

The other day we were shown a relic of the olden times of a very singular character. It consists of a small parcel of some kind of grass or swampy shrub, twisted over which in the form of a cross are two horse-shoe nails, the whole bound together by red thread passing over the centre of the nails. This is, we believe, an ancient form of the charm or amulet. The relic in question was found by Mr Mackay, plumber, above the door-lintel of an old house in Castle Street, which he is at present engaged in demolishing. The building is a very old one, situated immediately below the old mansion-house of the lairds of Inshes, and the charm was doubtless put in the place where it was found by some superstitious inhabitant of the dwelling at a very early period. (*IA*, 7 June 1859)

In the summer of 1939, the Inverness papers were concerned mainly about school sports days, tourists, and the generally undistinguished life and events in a small market town, though there were occasional references to national politics and the deteriorating international situation. People were well aware of Hitler and the threat he posed. Locally, the council were making preparations to start work on a new bridge, replacing the Suspension Bridge. One citizen had had enough of their high-handed approach:

REPLACING SUSPENSION BRIDGE

Sir, – Our Town Council take such high-handed actions these days that one is inclined to suspect that there is some unknown influence guiding or *dictating* every action, and I am sure many people share my belief that we have a dictator – that is to say we have an official who not only thinks he is a dictator, but has been able to convince the Inverness Town Council that they are the minor partners of this axis.

The latest aggression against an already fed-up public has been the closing of Huntly Steeet and forcing traffic to use what would appear to be a private road near the Glenalbyn Hotel and other properties, much to the danger of pedestrians who are also forced to use this roadway.

However, it would appear that the proprietors of this roadway are a very tolerant or suppressed lot, and so far have not complained or taken defensive action. Such action, I am sure, would force the aggressor to open at least one part of Huntly Street, which is really very wide at the part in question, and I am sure could both serve the traffic needs of the community and also accommodate the plant of the bridge engineers.

Our traffic problem is already to be deplored, and I do hope that this letter will not be the cause of inflicting another one-way street on the poor motorist, who has already to dodge Church Street, Bank Street and Hamilton Street. – Yours etc

DISGUSTED

(*IC*, 25 July 1939)

It is interesting to see the language of the time impinging on everyday life.

This letter did not go unnoticed and soon another citizen added his thoughts:

BRIDGE STREET SCHEME

Sir, – I read with interest "Disgusted's" letter in Tuesday's issue, and certainly share his belief that our Civic Fathers are under some sort of Dictator influence, and to all intents and purposes appear content to allow this influence to control their decisions. With the construction of the new bridge we see what is, in my opinion, an abuse of the powers vested in local authorities by the compulsory purchase provisions of certain Acts.

Yesterday a scheme was announced for the redevelopment of Bridge Street, and as the shopkeepers and others who are to lose their premises have not yet been informed of the fate in store for them, the redevelopment plan is, in my opinion, premature. The scheme referred to actually concerned the ground which *would not actually* be required for road widening, and upon which I fail to see how the local authority can apply the order, at least honestly. The duty of our Councillors is to protect the ratepayer, and most of the people concerned are double ratepayers, and if none of our Councillors make a stand in their interests I would like to see shopkeepers and others who are being displaced make some sort of collective action against this aggression. United they would at least receive more respect, and might be able to convince the Council that before any form of rede-velopment is planned, each and every person displaced should have his, or her, individual needs embraced in the scheme. – Yours etc.,

DISGUSTED TOO

(*IC*, 28 July 1939)

On 11 August 1939 the *Courier* reported the visit of a German fishery cruiser, the *Weser*; it had visited on three previous occasions, enjoying typical Highland hospitality from the British Legion and civic authorities, but this time they had a much cooler welcome. The crew of sixty were described as Nazis, who were interested to hear that on the day before their arrival the Prime Minister, Neville Chamberlain, had passed through Inverness while on holiday in the Highlands. The Highland Pageant entertained crowds for four days at the Northern Meeting Park. The Magistrates announced that Castle Road would be closed from 23 August until 11 September to allow for the demolition of property at the end of Bridge Street so that a temporary roadway could be made to connect with the Temporary Bridge which would carry traffic over the Ness while the old Suspension Bridge was demolished and the new bridge constructed. Of course, world events intervened and it would be twenty years before these carefully laid plans were put into effect. After the declaration of war with Germany on 3 September 1939 the Town Clerk, Mr James Cameron, announced that plans for the demolition of the Suspension Bridge on 11 September would be shelved. An official letter from the Ministry of Transport duly arrived later in the month.

But in the meantime, on 25 August the *Inverness Courier* reported on progress:

THE NEW BRIDGE

Demolition of Old Buildings

Some Interesting Finds

Rapid progress is now being made with the preliminary work of the demolition of the Suspension Bridge, Inverness, which, as stated in our last issue, will be closed for traffic from 11th September. The temporary staging on piles across the river on the north side of the bridge has been completed and the first of the large cranes which will deal with the work of demolition of the bridge is now in process of erection.

A further stage has been reached with the making of the approach to the Castle Road, which has now been closed temporarily until the corner house on Bridge Street has been demolished and a new roadway made leading to the Temporary Bridge. The roadway, it is expected, will be completed by the 11th September. When more properties in Bridge Street are acquired the temporary roadway will be moved somewhat nearer to the Castle wall so as to allow the abutments of the new bridge to be erected.

On the west side of the river the demolition work on the Glenalbyn Hotel is well towards completion. The present footpath from Young Street to Huntly Street will continue to be available. Young Street will be closed for vehicular traffic when the work starts on the bridge on 11th September. On each side of the street, however, there will be footpaths, one to Huntly Street and the other to Ness Walk.

A LATIN QUOTATION

It is interesting to learn that several finds have been made in course of the demolition of the Glenalbyn Hotel, which was probably erected in the middle of the seventeenth century. It was found that a large number of river boulders were used in the buildings. The wood-work, despite its age, was in fairly good condition. The joists, instead of being fastened by ordinary rails, were held in position by oak pins. On one of the long oak beams an inscription was scratched. It was at first thought that the words were in Gaelic. After careful study, however, on the part of Mr A. B. Peters, librarian, assisted by a former Royal Academy pupil, Mr Joseph Alistair Duthie, now at St Andrews University, the writing was found to be a Latin quotation from Horace (Book I., **XVIII.**) The inscription reads: –

"Nam tua res agitur, paries cum proximus ardet";

Which can be translated thus: –

"For your interests are at stake when your neighbour's house is on fire."

The beam, it is to be hoped, will be preserved, and find a home in the Inverness Museum.

Another interesting find in the Glen Albyn Hotel buildings was a marriage stone dated 1846. The stone bears the coat of arms of Forbes of Culloden – three bears; heads and a crescent.

HISTORY OF CASTLE TOLMIE

It is a curious coincidence that when the operations to erect the present Suspension Bridge were begun in 1852 a large pile of buildings, known as Castle Tolmie, had to be removed. The new buildings erected afterwards and known as Castle Tolmie are now to be demolished under the present scheme. (*IC*, 25 August 1939)

It was thought that the name Tolmie derived from a family of that name who occupied the site in the early 1800s. Built in 1678, the same year as the stone bridge which was swept away in the 1849 floods, it was the town residence of Forbes of Culloden for many years. By 1822 it had deteriorated markedly and was described as 'a third or fourth-rate inn', with demolition proposed then. However, it survived for another thirty years.

MUSIC HALL

One of the great venues in Inverness for all manner of public meetings and entertainments was the Music Hall on Union Street, later the Methodist

Church, which burned down on 7 December 1961. John Wesley himself had visited Inverness in 1770, and in 1797 Methodists opened a chapel at the end of Inglis Street. Mainly because of lack of space they bought the Music Hall in 1922, paying £7,000 to convert it for ecclesiastical use. They moved to a brand new church on the west side of the river in 1965, after the fire in the Music Hall.

The Music Hall opened in 1865 and quickly became the prime venue for a wide range of activities. The Gaelic Society of Inverness held its meetings there; the Inverness Choral Union used it for its concerts; there were Fine Arts exhibitions, the annual Poultry & Bird Show, a baby show, a cycling exhibition, political meetings, including suffragists and the Great Liberal Demonstrations in 1885, 1886 and 1887, Christmas pantomimes, and many lectures, including George Mallory, speaking about the impending 1922 Everest expedition, Arthur Conan Doyle on 'Facts about Fiction' (1893), General Booth of the Salvation Army (1901), Dr Barnardo on 'Destitute Children' (1876), and the novelist Annie S. Swan (1922).

Among the highlights over the years were concerts on behalf of the Indian Famine Fund (1900), the Boy Scouts, the Working Men's Club library, the Children's Free Breakfast Fund, and The Clachnacuddin Lodge of Oddfellows. 'Moving Photographs' arrived in 1896. The Inverness Abstainers' Union Christmas concert (1865) was one of the first fund-raising events. The Music Hall was the venue for annual dinners, for example of the Northern Counties Cricket Club; and for the employees of the Rose Street Foundry. Perhaps The Laughing Gas Company, who performed in the Music Hall in 1877, would fall foul of health and safety regulations today. The Jubilee Singers, an African-American *a cappella* ensemble from Fisk University, in Nashville, Tennessee, performed in 1900, while the Christy Minstrels visited in 1866 and 1874; Scott Skinner, the Strathspey King, gave a concert in the Music Hall, at the age of 80, in full Highland dress, to a 'crowded audience', on 13 May 1922. The Salvation Army even held a wedding in the Music Hall, in 1886. Haydn's *The Creation* (1880), was one of many memorable concerts.

Even after it became the Wesleyan Hall, it continued to be used as a cultural venue – the Glasgow Orpheus Choir, conducted by Hugh Roberton, performed there in April 1924. The Scottish Philharmonic Orchestra used it for a broadcast concert in 1932. The Inverness Light Opera Company performed *The Gondoliers* there in 1934.

The Grand Opening of the Music Hall in 1865 was well advertised:

INVERNESS, WEDNESDAY, JULY 26th

GRAND OPENING CONCERT IN THE NEW MUSIC HALL

MR MORINE has the honour to announce
that he has succeeded in engaging the following
celebrated Artistes for the above important occasion: –

MRS and MR W. HOWARD

(Late leasee of the Edinburgh Operetta House)

and

MR T. MACLAGAN

who will give selections from their

PORTFOLIO MUSICALE and COMIC

SKETCH BOOK,

Comprising Vocal, Instrumental and Humorous
Illustrations;

Also the eminent Scottish Tenor

MR A. MILNE

Conductor – MR MORINE.

Reserved Seats (limited number), 3s; Front Seats, 2s;
Body of the Hall, 1s.

Doors open at half-past Seven. Concert to commence
At Eight.

Full particulars in Programmes to be had at the
Booksellers.

This event was of course covered extensively in the local papers:

OPENING OF UNION STREET MUSIC HALL – GRAND CONCERT

The handsome new public hall in Union Street was opened on the evening of Wednesday last by a grand concert, under the management of Mr Morine, late of Inverness, when several musical celebrities were introduced. The hall was well filled, about five hundred persons being present. Before the proceedings of the evening commenced, Mr Morine intimated that Mr Charles Stewart, who had been the chief promoter of the Music Hall, had kindly consented to preside on the occasion.

Mr Stewart, who retained his place in the body of the hall, addressed a few words of congratulation to those present on the opening of the building. He referred to its happy conception and successful completion, and trusted it would help to promote the comfort, convenience, amusement, and instruction of the citizens of Inverness. The town was not always so prosperous as it is at present; it had long suffered from the depressing influence of a series of disasters, from which it first revived by the successful establishment of the Caledonian Bank. Then came the Inverness and Nairn Railway, and since then railways had been extended in all directions, until it might now be confidently expected that Inverness would recover the trade which Glasgow had taken from her on the one hand and Aberdeen on the other. The evidence of prosperity was never so visible. Look at the handsome streets that were springing up in every direction, at the villas in the neighbourhood, at the educational institutions of the town, that might compare with any in all broad Scotland – look at the street in which they now met, which was a credit to the gentlemen, natives of Inverness, by whom it was carried out. (Cheers.) It was in these circumstances that the erection of a Music Hall was projected, and never had any undertaking been more warmly supported. He trusted that it would conduce not only to the amusement, but to the instruction of the people, especially to the youth of the town, for whom he hoped systematic lectures on literary and scientific subjects would be organised. (Cheers.) The lads of Inverness of this generation would be the men of the next, and it depended on how they were educated, how they would perform their part. If the erection of this hall contributed in any way to their improvement, he was sure the shareholders would feel themselves well repaid (Applause.) (*IA*, 28 July 1865)

Leaving aside commentary on the actual performances, it is interesting that the *Inverness Advertiser* gives a detailed description of the building itself:

It affords us satisfaction to state, from the trial of the hall just made, that it has been found to be admirably adapted for the purpose of musical entertainments; and indeed, if there is any fault at all to find, it is that the place sounds too well, there being a slight reverberation or echo, which to some extent affects the clearness of the sound, particularly noticeable in the vocal performances. The hall itself is a plain but elegant structure in the classic style, from designs by Mr Alexander Ross, architect, Inverness, exhibiting an external length of 100 feet, divided into three compartments, those in the extremities being 25 feet in length, and projecting in front of the central portion to the extent of about eighteen inches. The first floor of the building contains four large shops with commodious cellars underneath, and separated by massive piers of rusticated stonework. On the second flat is the hall, the front of which is divided into seven bays by pilasters, having arched windows between, each 22 feet high, and filled with polished plate glass. The façade is carried several feet higher than the adjoining buildings, and is finished with a cornice and balustrade. The entrance to the hall is in the centre, the passage being 12 feet wide, and the doorway ornamented by a balcony with richly-carved trusses. At the end of the passage is a broad flight of seven steps, at the top of which, stairs break off to the right and left, and conduct to the hall. On entering here, the visitor is at once struck with the spaciousness and beauty of the interior, and with the chasteness characterising the execution of the various decorations. The hall is capable of accommodating from 1000 to 1100 persons, and, were a gallery erected at the east end could hold easily 1300. It is 90 feet long, including the orchestra, 44 feet wide and 32 feet high, having a deep cornice with modillions and coved up to the ceiling, in which are placed three sunlights, the approved mode of nightly illumination, each of which contains 96 burners, and is surrounded with mouldings and ornaments of the form of a star. At the west end are the orchestra and stage, with easy access to them from ladies' and gentlemen's retiring rooms behind, to the left and right, and over them is a large apartment, suitable as a cloak room, measuring 44 by 15 feet. Precaution has been taken to provide against the emergency of a sudden pressure or crush, by the formation of a means of exit additional to the front entrance, opening into the Market Court. Altogether the structure is most creditable to the architect, an ornament to the town of Inverness, and its erection most commendable – as we hope it will prove profitable – to those of the community who have a financial interest in its success.

Northern Meeting Rooms

The Northern Meeting Rooms building has been described as 'a large plain structure.' The symmetrical frontage onto Church Street had originally a columned portico projecting over the pavement. As to the internal decoration of the premises, we know that in 1821 seven cut-glass chandeliers were erected in the Meeting Rooms at a cost of £700. The *Inverness Journal* of 14 September 1821 thought that the 'elegant chandeliers' were welcome 'additional embellishments.' They remained in the building until it was demolished, when they were given on permanent loan to the Town Council who used three of them to adorn the Council Chamber and one to light the main staircase in the Town House. The others were reportedly kept in storage and used as necessary to replace damage.

In 1833 it is reported that the ground floor of the Northern Meeting Rooms 'has been recently fitted up, and really makes a commodious and shewy theatre.' The opening production was 'Rob Roy', followed by 'The Bride of Lammermoor' and 'Tom Thumb'. The *Inverness Courier* was more interested in the leading actress, Mrs Ryder: 'She is really an extremely interesting and impressive actress, with great tact and tenderness,' and 'deserving of particular mention.' (*IC*, 17 April 1833)

The Rooms were closed in 1962, though demolition was delayed until 1966. The *Highland News* for 19 May 1966 had an interesting article on the subject:

FROM ROYAL GRANDEUR TO RUBBLE

Within a matter of three or four days now, two relics of the Northern Meeting Rooms – relics that are worth a considerable sum, quite apart from their value to the Community as a memento of the grandeur that made the Northern Meeting Ball the focal point in the Highland social calendar for many years – are destined to oblivion under the harsh blows of the demolisher's hammer.

It is almost seven years since the Northern Meeting Rooms, now only a drab reminder of past occasions, was sold for some sort of development. Recently the demolition gangs moved in to reduce the building – and not a few hearts with it – to rubble.

To the average Invernessian, the Northern Meeting Ball was a splendid occasion, strictly for the 'landed gentry,' but to which hundreds flocked as onlookers, as one or another of the Royal Family arrived.

The relics due to come under the hammer within a few days are steeped in nostalgia as reminders of the past – a past that may well be forgotten if nothing is done to change the fate of a wrought iron balcony and a solid oak balustrade.

RARE RELIC

Starting at the top – for that is where the demolition began – the balcony, exquisitely fashioned, as former devotees of the dance floor will remember, has probably only a slight monetary value. But as a relic of the past and its association with royalty it is a rarity.

The balustrade, has been partly removed already – one part by an amateur woodcarver, who realised that the value of the wood was too great to leave it for the 'hammer'. The solid oak of the balustrade, still in remarkably excellent condition, is worth more than £1,000 – if you could buy it today at all.

IRONIC

What then could be done with these items – if they are salvaged? It was perhaps ironic that at the same time as the demolition workers were 'hard at it,' only a matter of 100 yards away, Inverness Town Council's Parks and Cemeteries Committee were also busy discussing the proposed new Sports Centre at Queen's Park. Ironic, in as much as one of the topics was the cost of the new centre, which will include a dance hall. It would not be out of the way then to suggest that the very fine balustrade at the Northern Meeting Rooms could be adapted to the needs of the new Sports Centre. It would seem a matter of adjusting the design plans to accommodate £1000 worth of fittings which would serve as a memento of the past – and provide as fine a staircase as could be imagined for the Sports Centre.

The balcony, though, presents another problem. For all its beauty as a showpiece, it is hardly likely that it could be used as an integral part of the new centre.

But the wrought iron work, with a suitable plaque, might provide an attractive exterior showpiece, to give the new some real connection with the old.

A SHAME

We asked Mr George MacBean, Inverness Registrar, whether he thought there was a case for preserving these relics. "It would be a shame to put a hammer through that lovely iron-work and the valuable balustrade," he said. He added: "It would be rather nice if there was some way in which they could be accepted by an organisation – such as the Town Council – for there must be some suitable use for them."

From the point of view of many of the hundreds in the Highlands who have attended the Ball at some time or other, the preservation of the balcony would be welcome news. Especially if it were to be placed in the successor to the Northern Meeting Rooms, at the new centre at the Queen's Park. And the same can be said of the balustrade, which though old is far from out of date.

But all is not lost – yet! Mr George Campbell, of Messrs James Campbell Construction Ltd, Tomnahurich Street, who are demolition contractors at the Northern Meeting Rooms, told us: "If anybody wants these items they have only to get in touch with me. But it will have to be soon, because the work on demolition must progress."

Mr Campbell made it quite clear that he would be only too happy to accommodate any genuine approach. But he felt that the cost of removal of the two relics might be hefty.

In spite of that, it seems a terrible pity that items of such intrinsic value should be doomed to destruction, in the near shell-like remains of that was once a right royal meeting place.

BALL

In Connection With

**THE HIGHLAND AND AGRICULTURAL SOCIETY'S
SHOW AT INVERNESS**

THIS BALL will be held within the **NORTHERN
MEETING ROOMS, INVERNESS,** on *Wednesday, the
2nd day of August next.*

Stewards.

The Lords-Lieutenants of the Counties embraced in the District of the Show.
The Members of Parliament of the Counties.
The Conveners of the Counties.
The Provosts of the Counties.

Ball Committee

The Honourable the Master of Lovat (Convener)
The Honourable Major James Grant of Grant
The Honourable Colonel Alister Fraser of Lovat.
Sir Alexander Gordon-Cumming, Bart. of Altyre.
J. Hall-Maxwell, Esq. of Dargavel, C. B.
D. Davidson, Esq. of Tulloch.
Aeneas Mackintosh, Esq. of Daviot.

H. W. White, Esq. of Monar.

Fountaine Walker, Esq. of Foyers.

Major Wardlaw, Belmaduthy.

Walter Carruthers, Esq. of Inverness.

Dancing to commence at Nine o'clock.

Supper and Refreshments to be under the charge of Mr
Macdonald of the "Peacock."

Ladies. Tickets of admission, 7s. 6d.; Gentlemen's Tickets,
12s. 6d.; to be had at the Inverness booksellers.

J. ANDERSON, 15 Union Street,

Hon. Secretary.

(*IC*, 27 July 1865)

This advertisement appeared on the front page of the *Courier* and left the
citizens of Inverness in no doubt that this was a glittering occasion; the price
of tickets excluded 95% of the Highland population. However, not to be
outdone, the organisers of the premier social occasion in the Highland social year, the Northern Meeting itself, also gave advance notice of their own
event, with the roll call of Stewards showing it to be an even more glittering
assemblage of aristocracy and landed gentry, and their ladies:

NORTHERN MEETING
(Instituted in 1788)

THE NORTHERN MEETING is to hold
this year on THURSDAY and FRIDAY, the *21st and 22nd
September next.*
The following Noblemen and Gentlemen are the OFFICE-
BEARERS for the present year, viz.: –

Patron.

His Grace the Duke of Richmond.

Permanent Steward.

The Right Hon. Lord Lovat.

Stewards.

The Right Hon. the Earl of Seafield.

The Right Hon. Lord Abinger.

The Hon. James Grant.

The Hon. Colonel Fraser, Master of Lovat.

The Hon. Colonel A. Fraser.

Sir Kenneth S. Mackenzie of Gairloch, Bart.

Sir A. P. Gordon-Cumming of Altyre, Bart.

General Sir Patrick Grant, G. C. B.

James Murray-Grant of Glenmoriston.

Seaforth.

Henry J. Baillie, yr. of Redcastle, M. P.

Major C. L. Cumming-Bruce of Roseisle, M. P.

Alexander Matheson of Ardross, M. P.

James Merry of Belladrum, M. P.

Dudley Coutts Marjoribanks of Guisachan, M. P.

Donald Cameron of Lochiel.

Cluny Macpherson.

Robert Bruce Aeneas Macleod of Cadboll.

Duncan Davidson of Tulloch.

Aeneas Mackintosh of Daviot.

Colonel Fraser-Tytler of Aldourie

John Fraser of Bunchrew.

Major James Wardlaw of Belmaduthy House.

Eneas W. Mackintosh of Raigmore.

Fountaine Walker of Foyers.

Henry W. White of Monar, and

The Provost of Inverness.

BALLS and SUPPERS, as usual, on *Thursday* and *Friday*
evenings.
COMPETITIONS of the NATIONAL MUSIC and HIGHLAND
GAMES and SPORTS will be held on the forenoons
of each of the days of the Meeting.
Particulars in future Advertisements.
HENRY W. WHITE, *Convener.*
Inverness, 10th July 1865.
(*IC*, 27 July 1865)

Returning to the Highland Agricultural Show, their Ball was scheduled for Wednesday 2 August, but on the night before they held their
annual banquet in the new Music Hall, with 'upwards of 450 gentlemen'
being present. In typical reportage of its time, the *Courier* gives a very full
account of proceedings, quoting many of the speeches in full, taking up five
full columns of text – a fascinating glimpse into mid-Victorian society. It
was a good night:

The proceedings terminated a few minutes before ten o'clock, every one present seeming to have been gratified with the successful character of the meeting, and the pleasing aspect of the whole gathering, which was enhanced by the clean and elegant interior and the brilliant lighting of the new hall. (*IC*, 3 August 1865)

Needless to say, ladies were not invited to the banquet – they were saving themselves for the Ball.

The Music Hall was destroyed by fire on 5 December 1898, as reported in the *Inverness Courier* on the following day:

The people of Inverness, on getting up yesterday morning, were startled by the news that the Music Hall had been burned down a few hours before. The fire had come and gone like a thief in the night, and the report, which had not obtained the currency of print, was barely credited; but a glance at the erstwhile handsome building, in the centre of the north side of Union Street, put the matter beyond doubt. There was nothing standing but the bare walls and the shop fronts below. The whole interior of the Hall, the floor and the roof had disappeared in the night, and the place, viewed from the top of a wall, looked like a great square pit, into which masses of debris, mostly charred pieces of wood and lengthy black beams, had been thrown by a remorseless hand. The heavy iron girder and the iron pillars which supported the balcony, odd pieces of the balcony rail, and some of the ornamental stanchions of the same metal which supported the gallery were all that remained, in addition to a part of the floor, with chairs and forms, along the front of the hall. The rest, which was practically the whole of the interior, had been reduced to a mass of tons upon tons of worthless debris. The shops and their valuable contents shared the same fate, and it is believed that the Hall buildings will have to rebuilt from the foundations.

It's not clear what caused this conflagration. The United Temperance Committee had concluded what was described as a 'Pleasant Saturday Evening' and the caretaker had locked up as usual by 11 pm on the Saturday night. The *Courier* added some commentary about the finances of the operation and the premises affected at Nos 26-36 Union Street:

We have given an account of the ruined condition to which the Hall – the only really good and capacious Hall in the town – has been reduced. It was the property of the Inverness Music Hall Company, to which Mr W. T. Rule, solicitor, is secretary. The fabric was insured with the Alliance Company for the sum of £5,500, and the furniture, fixtures, galleries, &c., for £800, the rents being separately insured for £500. The four firms who were tenants of the Company in the basement shops have also suffered grievous loss, and, like the proprietors of the Hall, they are deprived of the use of their premises. The ceilings of three of the shops – Messrs Cowan and Co. (Mr Campbell), wine merchants; Messrs A. & S. Fraser, drapers; and Mr Henry Mitchell, chemist – were smashed through by the falling debris and the fire penetrated into them and consumed a great part of the stocks-in-trade. What was not actually destroyed by the fire was broken up by falling beams and pieces of iron, or rendered worthless by the flood of water which poured upon them. The ceiling of the shop of Messrs Bookless Bros., successors to Freeman & Co., fish and game dealers, at the east end of the Hall buildings, was preserved intact but the water percolated through it in great quantities, and the goods were removed in a sodden condition. In every case, fortunately, the stock-in-trade was insured, but, as the merchants will have to find other premises, their loss will be very great. The situation is one of the most central in the town and vacant places are not easily found in the locality. Some other people have shared in the general loss by the fire. The numerous telephone wires, which passed over the Hall, were broken up and twisted about in the most fantastic manner. The value of these wires, and the cost of replacing them has to be borne by the National Telephone Company. In the Hall were a piano and organ which the United Temperance Company had hired from Messrs Logan & Co. Both instruments were destroyed. Taking everything into account, the actual damage done by the fire is calculated to amount to considerably over £10,000.

The Music Hall, which has well served a generation of Invernessians in providing excellent accommodation for all sorts of entertainments, was opened on 7th July 1865, the opening entertainment taking the seasonable form of a flower show. The Hall was designed to form a component part of the fine line of Union Street then erected. It was built to the order of a company, the promoters of which were the late Mr Charles Stewart, Mr Rule, the present secretary, and Dr Alex. Ross. The latter gentleman was the architect of the Hall, and it has been erected, has existed, and has been destroyed by fire in the course of his long professional career. The building covered a site 100 feet in length and 60 feet in width. It was a handsome structure, with a smart frontage in the classic style and lighted from Union Street by seven tall arched windows. The entrance was in the centre and there were two shops on each side. In 1880 the comfort and capacity of the Hall were greatly increased by improvements, including the erection of a balcony which traversed three sides of the interior and was broadened into a wide gallery at the east end. The platform and orchestra filled up the other extremity, with two small anterooms beneath the orchestra seats. For nearly twenty years the Hall was not in great demand and it barely paid its way. The shop rents afterwards rose until they nearly doubled themselves, and, with the growing increase in the number of entertainments, the return was more lucrative. Recently, the property has yielded a dividend of six or seven per cent. per annum. We have no doubt that the Directors are quite alive to what were generally considered shortcomings in the Hall, as, for instance, the very limited retiring accommodation, and it may be taken for granted that in replacing the Hall, they will introduce the latest improvements and provide, as they did in the past, a concert hall which will answer the requirements of the community.

On the following Saturday night, the United Temperance Committee met in the Theatre Royal for its regular 'Pleasant Saturday Evening' entertainment, attracting a large audience and producing takings which exceeded those made in the Music Hall.

Initially there were rumours that the Music Hall would be rebuilt from the original plans and specifications, but these proved unfounded.

The *Inverness Courier* of 17 October 1899 contains a good description of the new Music Hall, which since it was in turn destroyed by fire in 1961, is worth reproducing:

THE NEW MUSIC HALL

AN ATTRACTIVE BUILDING

The reconstruction of the Music Hall, in Union Street, is rapidly approaching completion, and the new Hall will be opened with a concert by the Choral Union on Friday, 10th November, when, as we understand, a befitting ceremony will precede the music. The new Hall is an immense improvement on the old hall, which, barring the masonry, was destroyed by fire. Owing to the limitations of the site, the general scheme is the same; in details, many improvements have been effected, and the fitting and finishing in hall, anterooms, corridors, and stairways have been carried out in an ornate and artistic manner, rendering the Hall very much more pleasing and attractive, as well as more comfortable, than it had been before. The principal entrance has been doubled in width, and, with the collapsible gates at the street and a close screen and doors at the inner end, it will form a roomy vestibule, thirty feet long and fifteen feet wide. The flooring of the vestibule is laid with tiles, and, to the height of five feet, the walls are finished in cream-coloured tiles with appropriate base and borders. Beyond the vestibule doors, the entrance stairs are divided for the front seat and back seat patrons, who will procure their tickets at separate sides of the box-office. Stone stairs lead in both directions to the Hall and galleries, thus making stone the means of egress from all parts of the Hall. The access to the orchestra and galleries has been widened and otherwise improved.

The interior of the Hall is practically new in every respect, and, though necessarily having a general resemblance to the old Hall, its stately lines have been beautified out of all recognition. To ensure plenty of light in the day-time, three large cupola window lights have been opened in the roof, and they divide the ceiling into imposing panels with beams and mullions. The design of the ceiling, artistically finished in colours, adds much to the beauty of the Hall. The windows facing Union Street have been glazed with plate glass. These windows are doubled, which will prevent draughts when parts are opened, and will deaden the noises from the street. At night the hall will be lit throughout with electric light, which will improve both its appearance and its temperature. The seating accommodation of the Hall is the same as formerly. For the extension of the platform a row of seats has been taken from the front of the area, but it is compensated for by the addition of a row to the gallery. The platform is larger, and it can be doubled in extent by the simple device of drawing out an extension which rests below. Those who have had occasion to use the old platform for "demonstration" purposes will appreciate this particular improvement more almost than any other.

The new retiring rooms at the back of the platform are large and comfortable apartments. An independent passage immediately behind the platform gives separate access to these rooms, and forms a useful connection between both sides of the Hall. The gentlemen's room is on the south side, next Union Street, and the ladies' room adjoins the entrance stairs. The two sets of lavatory accommodation – that for the gentlemen being on an upper level at the rear of the building – are of the latest type, and the floors and walls are laid with tiles and beautifully finished.

On the whole, we have no hesitation in congratulating the proprietors and the architects (Messrs Ross & Macbeth) on the splendid use to which they have put the space at their disposal, and on having provided a Hall which will be of public advantage to the town. It is to be hoped that nothing will be permitted in the Hall that will detract from its comfort and tasteful appearance as a concert and lecture room. It is said on good authority that the proprietary Company were disposed to contemplate in a favourable light the erection of a pipe organ; but alterations which they had to make, willy-nilly, in the front entrance and stairway, and, as a consequence, in the adjoining shops and foundations, necessitated the expenditure of £600 more than had been bargained for, and the organ was dropped. It is a proposal, however, which the proprietors of the Hall do not intend to lose sight of altogether. It is to be hoped not in the interests of good music for the people. Whilst we are about it, we should also congratulate the contractors on the excellence of their work. The contractors are: – Mason, Geo. Bain; carpenter, D. Maclennan; slater, Alex. Fraser; plasterer, John Macphee; plumbers, Thomson & Co.; painters, Wm. Ross & Son; blacksmith and tile and heating work, Rose Street Foundry Coy.; electric lighting, P. C. Middleton & Co. Mr John Ross has efficiently performed the duties of clerk of works.

The Music Hall reopened on Friday 10 November 1899. The inaugural concert was well-attended and well-received, and in the following weeks it was the venue for many other events, perhaps most notably a patriotic concert on behalf of the servicemen fighting in 'the Transvaal War' in South Africa.

In 1922 the premises were acquired by the Methodist church – their premises in Inglis Street were not big enough. The cost of buying and renovating the Music Hall was £7,000.

Methodist Church
PURCHASE OF MUSIC HALL

The Methodist congregation have acquired the Music Hall in Union Street, which they propose transforming into their place of worship. The congregation have been hampered for years by the very limited seating accommodation of their church at Inglis Street, and it is thought that the Music Hall, centrally situated, can be converted easily into a commodious and suitable edifice. At a meeting of the trustees and congregation of the Methodist connection, it was agreed unanimously to purchase the Music Hall. It was also agreed to retain the present church buildings in Inglis Street as a hall for the Sabbath School and meetings. A letter was read from Mr Donald Mitchell, senior steward, regretting his inability to be present at the meeting, and warmly approving of the proposal to purchase the Music Hall. It was stated that Mr Mitchell was to be married on the following day, and the meeting sent congratulations to him and his bride.

The proposal to acquire the Music Hall was heartily entered into by Rev. Mr Kedward, the popular minister of the congregation. Mr Kedward's term of office here as minister should terminate in September, but it has been resolved by the congregation to retain Mr Kedward for another year. The cost of purchasing the Music Hall and renovating the hall and present church is estimated at over £7000. (*IC*, 2 June 1822)

It took until 1926 for the conversion to be completed and the building continued in their ownership until another disastrous fire which once again destroyed it completely, in 1961. The *Courier* gave a very full account of the 'disastrous' fire, but surprisingly little information about the history of the building, which was completely gutted and had to be demolished immediately. The only thing to survive the fire was the baptismal font. The *Courier* was facing its print deadline, for the fire took place early on the morning of Friday 8 December 1961 and was reported in the issue published later that day. They were able to mention that:

The premises were purchased and converted into a church in 1926 – and many townspeople have ever since been critical of the Town Council for not purchasing the property, the controversy which raged at the time being furious.

By their next issue, on 12 December 1961, the *Courier* could update its readers:

AFTERMATH OF CHURCH FIRE
Tons of Debris Being Removed

Workmen yesterday continued to remove debris from the Inverness Methodist Church which was completely destroyed by fire early on Thursday morning. The work of clearing the shell that remains of the Church and making the walls of the building safe has been entrusted to Messrs James Campbell and Son, builders, Inverness, and to facilitate the dangerous task they have erected derricks on Union Street, which has been closed to vehicles in the interest of public safety. When the tons of debris are removed – it was being taken out yesterday by teams of workmen who tipped it out in barrow-loads from the arched windows into lorries on the street below – and when some charred beams have been taken from the roof, it will probably be found necessary to demolish some of the walls.

Noting that the damage done in the 1898 fire was estimated at the time at £10,000, the *Courier* suggested that the damage this time 'was probably ten times that amount.'

All this was of course happening at the same time as the demolitions on Bridge Street were about to get under way. Meanwhile, the *Highland News* had the fire as front page news on its issue of Friday 8 December, with a dramatic photograph of the exterior, showing the distinctive arched windows silhouetted against a fiery background. By their next issue, they were ready for some reminiscing:

By the way…
Notes by "Nessian"

If you are in search of a perfect building line, and also some admirable examples of architecture, pay a visit some quiet evening, when cars are parked on both sides of it, to Union Street, Inverness, scene of the fire which destroyed the only Methodist Church in the burgh. It is indeed a perfect building line, and all the more to be admired because Union Street was built in the pre-planning age. And there were real talented architects in those days.

Union Street was built in 1861–64. It was previously a somewhat unenviable aggregation of "houses", [and would be seen as unfit] by today's standard requirements, alike by the Department of Health for Scotland and the Dean of Guild Court.

The four persons who were responsible for providing Inverness with its loveliest street were Charles Fraser MacKintosh, M. P. for Inverness burghs (and a prolific writer, on Highland and historic and antiquarian affairs), Donald Davidson, who became Sheriff of the island of Lewis, George C. MacKay, who later settled in Vancouver Island, and Hugh Rose, a well-known local solicitor.

The two largest buildings in Union Street are the Royal Hotel which occupies almost, or more than one half of the north side, and, on the south side, the former premises of A. Fraser and Co. (now Benzies).

Part of the north side is occupied by the Bank of Scotland. In those days the big banks also made housing provision for accommodating the manager and his family in the bank itself. But this custom is almost, if not entirely, no longer followed.

The old Caledonian Bank in High Street (now the Bank of Scotland), the British Linen Bank, High Street, the Commercial Bank, Church Street, the National Bank (for many years in Church Street), the Union Street branch of the Bank of Scotland – all had housing accommodation for their managers or agents.

MUSIC HALL

Before the three cinemas in the town centre were built, the Music Hall (which was owned by a private company) and the Market Hall were in great demand for political meetings, particularly the former. Here, the big guns of the Liberal and Tory Parties boomed in support of candidates. Lord Aberdeen Asquith and Ramsay MacDonald were among a host of notable politicians who spoke in the Music Hall, and ex-Premier Arthur Balfour in the Market Hall.

Lloyd George was another visitor, but on this occasion – again in the Music Hall – it was not Party politics but the future of the Gaelic language.

And it was in the Music Hall in 1929 that the Duke of York (afterwards King George VI) received the Freedom of the Burgh.

For amateur theatricals, in which the locals won their spurs, the old Music Hall was a useful training ground. There were visiting artists like Doctor Walford Bodie (mesmerist and ventriloquist) and merry-maker Funny Frame. Add to this the fine performances by Inverness Choral Union under the leadership of Mr Roddie.

CINEMA JOHN

The Music Hall had also been used for a variety of purposes, including Fancy Dress Balls and a memorable series of Sunday evening meetings by the Rev. Howard May, a celebrated minister of the Methodist Church, whose oratory ensured crowded attendances.

These memories of the Music Hall recall the first "pictures on the screen" shown locally; they were all "stills," of course, of local photographs which John MacKenzie, a well-known Invernessian, had taken himself. And the "show" was called – "As Others See Us."

John MacKenzie was the pioneer of cinematography in Inverness, and he found a much larger field for his talents when he went to Hollywood. (*HN*, 15 Dec 1961)

THEATRE ROYAL

The earliest theatre in Inverness was built in 1822, in what was then a location known as 'Castle Raat', renamed as Theatre Lane. This is now Hamilton Street, reduced to an alley at the west side of the Eastgate Centre.

This was the Theatre Royal. Nineteenth-century newspapers also give its location as Inglis Street, which runs parallel to Hamilton Street, suggesting that the theatre building spanned two streets. It seems to have closed, or more likely moved to a new location, in 1827.

Certainly, in 1882, a new Theatre Royal was built in Bank Street. The architects were Matthews and Lawrie. The *Inverness Advertiser* described it as 'classic Glasgow style'. The circular auditorium seated 750, with private boxes, a dress circle, orchestra stalls, a pit and a gallery. An operating licence was granted by the Justices of the Peace in October 1882 and from then until it burned down in March 1931 it was the main theatrical venue in the town.

The Theatre Royal was renovated in 1919, when electric lighting was installed and some improvements carried out – the dress circle and boxes were extended and upholstered. Much of the detail of performances and performers at the Theatre Royal over the years can be found in James Miller's account: *The Magic Curtain: The Story of Theatre in Inverness* (1986). Miller records that the final show was the famous comedian Will Fyfe, who opened on Monday 16 March 1931. Early on the Tuesday morning a fire broke out and was discovered about 1 a.m. The fire raged for three hours, but despite the best efforts of the fire brigade, who pumped water from the river, the theatre was completely destroyed, leaving what the *Northern Chronicle* described as "a mass of ugly black mire". Thankfully Tom, the theatre cat, was saved.

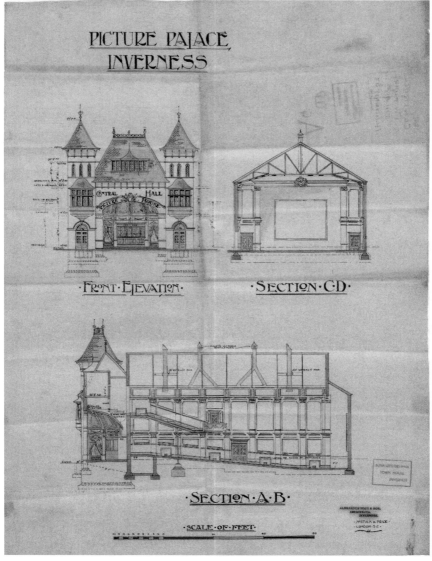

Plans and elevation of the Central Hall Picture House, later the Empire Theatre.

Inverness was left without a theatre until Sir Harry Lauder opened the new Empire Theatre in Academy Street on 17 September 1934, converted from its earlier role as a cinema (the Central Hall Picture House). It had accommodation for 1,000 people and impressed the *Northern Chronicle*:

> The outstanding feature of the reconstructed building is, of course, the stage. The wide and well-proportioned proscenium with the gorgeous draw curtain looks well from the front and the stage itself is equipped with the latest serviceable gadgets . . . The permanent drapings are handsome and practical, a drop cloth showing a realistic, if startlingly clean, representation of High Street.

By the 1960s, the advent of television and declining audiences, along with more stringent fire regulations, were putting the Empire Theatre under continuing pressure, and on 28 November 1970, with a rousing Gala Final Night, attended by over 1,000 people, it closed for good. It was demolished in September 1971 to make way for an office block.

Amateur dramatics continued to flourish in the renovated Arts Centre at Farraline Park (now the public library), soon renamed the Little Theatre, which opened on 6 January 1971. In December 1971 the Town Council launched a public appeal for a new theatre complex, to be built on the riverside beside the cathedral and Bishop Eden's palace – Eden Court Theatre finally opened, after many problems and delays, on 16 April 1976.

On Thursday 25 January 2001 the La Scala cinema on Strother's Lane closed, leaving the Vue cinema at the out-of-town Inverness Retail Park, and Eden Court Theatre's film programme, as the only movie options. The La Scala too was demolished, replaced by blocks of flats with retail outlets on the ground floor. The Playhouse cinema, opened in 1929 on Academy Street, was destroyed by fire on 14 March 1972. The architects were R. Carruthers, Ballantyne and Taylor. Jimmy Nairn, the Inverness photographer, was manager of the Playhouse from 1941 to 1972.

CHAPTER 13

LEGACY

It seems fitting to conclude this study of the lost architecture of Inverness with a brief look at what is left. Star of the show is undoubtedly the Town House, dating from 1882. John Gifford describes it as 'Flemish-Baronial' and hints at architectural plagiarism on the part of the architects (Matthews and Lawrie) by noting its resemblance to Gilbert Scott's Albert Institute in Dundee (1864). Across the road is the Town Steeple (1792) and on High Street the outstanding building is the headquarters of the Caledonian Bank (1847), in more recent times the Bank of Scotland and now a pub.

The most prominent buildings in town are what is often referred to incorrectly as Inverness Castle: the Sheriff Court (1835) and Inverness Jail (1848), later the District Court. In front of the Sheriff Court is an attractive statue of Flora MacDonald and her faithful collie dog.

Union Street, laid out in 1863, survives largely intact, apart from the Music Hall; Queensgate (1884) has suffered the loss of the Victorian Post Office but has mostly survived in its late Victorian but architecturally undistinguished character. Church Street has suffered many changes, but has the two oldest buildings in Inverness, with Abertarff House (1593) and Dunbar's Hospital, built as an alms house by Provost Alexander Dunbar in 1668. Bow Court, sympathetically restored by William Glashan in 1972, dates from 1725.

The ecclesiastical architecture of the town is mixed. The Old High Church is a bit of a hodge-podge, with the tower dating from the sixteenth-century, though probably with earlier masonry, especially in the lower part. The Episcopal cathedral, St Andrew's, has been described as 'stodgy' by Gifford and was the cause of much uninformed speculation when Inverness achieved 'city' status, along the lines that it would have been regarded as a city years ago if only the intended spires had been completed. Most of the 'old' churches in the town are architecturally pleasing and most of the 'new' churches are not.

There are several outstanding public buildings surviving, some of them in modified or altered circumstances. The Northern Infirmary (1804) is now

(2013) the headquarters of the University of the Highlands and Islands (UHI), whose historical research has highlighted the rather dubious origins of much of the capital which paid for it, deriving from Caribbean plantations and Indian trading enterprise. The Northern Counties District Lunatic Asylum (1864) has survived fire and conversion for housing, as has the Poorhouse, more recently known as Hilton Hospital. The wretched headquarters of the Highland Council incorporates the Tudor architecture of Alexander Ross's Northern Counties Collegiate School (1876); hopefully it will survive when the 1963 architecture is demolished and the council offices relocated, as is planned. The Public Library at Farraline Park, built as Dr Bell's School (1841) and used for a variety of purposes over the years, has an attractive Doric portico and will surely survive when, at some point, no doubt far in the future, Inverness finally gets the modern library it deserves – according to national standards for public libraries it has half the floor space required for the excellent services it provides. Inverness High School (1934) is an interesting Art Deco design. New Century House, in the shadow of the Kessock Bridge, is the head office for the *Inverness Courier* and the *Highland News* and is an impressive office block.

Though largely unheralded and perhaps lost in the fog of consternation arising from the redevelopment of Bridge Street and Eastgate, the domestic architecture of Inverness is perhaps the most attractive feature of its townscape. Not just the wonderful villas of the Crown, Annfield Road, Culduthel Road and Island Bank Road, or of Drummond Crescent, Old Edinburgh Road, Southside Road and Stratherrick Road, and adjoining nooks and crannies, or the housing of Ness Bank, but also the more modest Douglas Row, the nineteenth-century developments on the west side of the river, and the Victorian artisan housing Up the Hill. There are some outstanding properties, though as ongoing residences they are unfortunately not usually susceptible to close inspection. It is certainly the residential properties of Inverness, rather than the town centre, which give the place its specific character and appeal.

Sadly, this praise cannot extend to post-war council housing, or to the dormitory suburban housing, from Scorguie to Balloch, in which the prevailing ethos is utilitarianism.

Very occasionally, new buildings appear, which buck the trend and exhibit outstanding design. A new glass restaurant on Huntly Street has divided local opinion; the new National Trust for Scotland visitor centre at Culloden Battlefield (2007) has won architectural awards from some and is loathed by others; and when you compare the Eastgate Centre (1983 and 2002) to its competitors at Inshes or the A96 Retail Park, the designers deserve credit for making an effort, amidst regret at what was lost in the process. Similarly, the reconstituted complex at Eden Court (2007) has both its detractors and its admirers, while the Highland Archive and Registration Centre (2009) at the Bught has been described as resembling a Stalinist prison – but has also won awards! Internally it is certainly an attractive place for study and research and is a state-of-the-art facility for the conservation and preservation of archival records. Maggie's Centre (2005), at Raigmore Hospital, has also won wide recognition.

Finally, Viewhill House, the home of Joseph Mitchell, remains at risk, the subject of a protracted planning dispute after suffering major fire damage. It is profoundly to be hoped that this important part of our historical legacy can be preserved, not so much for its architectural merit as for its association with such an important personage. If it turns out that demolition is unavoidable, we can at least hope that on such an important site in our townscape a worthy edifice will be erected.

THE GOOD OLD DAYS?

In 1841, in a report prepared by George Anderson for the Poor Law Commissioners, in the aftermath of the cholera epidemics of 1832 and 1834, the full horrors of the public health crisis in Inverness were laid bare. Part of the report is a contribution by Dr John Inglis Nicol, at the time the Provost of Inverness:

> Inverness is a nice town, situated in a most beautiful country, and with every facility for cleanliness and comfort. The people are, generally speaking, a nice people, but their sufferance of nastiness is past endurance. Contagious fever is seldom or ever absent; but for many years it has seldom been rife in its pestiferous influence. The people owe this more to the kindness of Almighty God than to any means taken or observed for its prevention. There are very few houses in town which can boast of either water-closet or privy; and only two or three public privies in the better part of the place exist for the great bulk of the inhabitants. Hence there is not a street, lane, or approach to it that is not disgustingly defiled at all times, so much so as to render the whole place an absolute nuisance. The *midden* is the chief object of the humble; and though enough of water for purposes of cleanliness may be had by little trouble, still

the ablutions are seldom – MUCK in doors and out of doors *must* be their portion. When cholera prevailed in Inverness, it was more fatal than in almost any other town of its population in Britain.

In the later years of the nineteenth century much of the problem housing was swept away, and the infrastructure of sound public health provided: water and sewerage. In the town centre, in the 1860s, large-scale maps of the town show that behind the imposing facades were the remnants of former times, often converted to stables – the nineteenth-century equivalent of car parks. Gradually these were all cleared away, and with the redevelopment of the town centre from the 1860s onwards, eventually replaced completely by 'modern' buildings. There were no howls of protest from Victorian conservationists about the loss of eighteenth-century buildings: all agreed that they could not be got rid of quickly enough.

The irony of the situation today, when conservationists strive to ensure the survival of buildings erected at the expense of the historic medieval and eighteenth-century buildings of Inverness, should serve as a warning that change is inevitable, and usually dictated by commercial considerations. The best we can often hope for is that wherever possible changes can incorporate the best of the past, by preserving the appearance of old buildings, while reconstructing the interiors, as happened with the renovation of the Queensgate Hotel, gutted by fire in 1982.

What is inexcusable is thoughtless change, the kind of architectural vandalism which ruined Bridge Street, Young Street, and much of Church Street and Castle Street, with unattractive, unimaginative, glass and concrete structures. Today's architects have shown that they are capable of designing appropriate and imaginative buildings which fit into the older townscape while providing the facilities required by modern Invernessians. So, the prospects are not entirely gloomy, though there are still battles to be fought.

In recent years, the prevailing architectural ambience of Inverness has been seemingly unabated expansion and house-building, often prompting bemusement from older Invernessians and depression from young couples struggling to break into the housing market. Inverness has become almost cosmopolitan, with languages and accents from most of the countries of eastern Europe and the Baltic states. Jim Miller, in his *Inverness* (2006), a comprehensive tome on the history of the town through the ages, has an elegant description of the town in the first decade of the twenty-first century:

Outside the town centre the newer districts form a series of concentric developments rather like the growth rings on some ancient
tree. The first circle contains the housing estates and villas of the
Victorian period – stolid and well built in stone – and beyond them
come the Council houses of the early nineteenth century, still solidly
constructed from largely local materials. The outer rings have sprung
up in the last thirty years and display architectural styles now uni-
versal throughout Britain. The old heart of the town, the triangle of
High Street/Academy Street/Church Street, with its interconnect-
ing labyrinth of lanes, has seen an exodus. Most of the old shops,
locally owned, have gone and in their place now stand branches of
nationally known chain stores. The Exchange has become just another stretch of pavement – the term itself is hardly to be heard. The
pedestrianised High Street is still busy enough but there has been
a shift of public life eastward, to the Eastgate Centre, and beyond
that to the spanking new Eastgate II. Built on the site of the railway
goods yards, auction mart and stock yards, Eastgate II opened in
2003. Part of the site had been a complex of industrial and wholesale
premises, originally constructed around Falcon Square, itself named
after the Falcon ironworks. The new Falcon Square is an open plaza,
graced by a statue by the sculptor Gerald Laing, reminiscent of a
market cross. On top of the column of sandy-coloured stone rears
a unicorn, hence the nickname for this piece of art of 'the prick on
a stick'. Inverness's old market cross still stands at the front of the
Town House, grown a little grubby since its restoration in 1900,
generally unnoticed, the unicorn's horn broken off near the base.

James Miller's book benefits greatly from extensive research in local
newspapers; a recurring theme in his chapters on the nineteenth century is
the place of accidental fires in the town centre as an agent of change. Sometimes the dense, compacted housing and workshops staged their own version
of urban renewal.

We have encountered in this book many descriptions of Inverness; we
close with an account by Elizabeth Isabella Spence, a tourist with a sensitive
nose, in her *Letters from the North Highlands* (1816):

Inverness stands at the foot of a magnificent amphitheatre of hills,
so picturesque and diversified in shape, as to form one of the finest
natural landscapes it is possible to imagine.

Inverness is the capital of the Highlands, and considered the only town, north of Aberdeen, of importance. It is large and populous but the idea I had formed of noble streets, and elegant houses, greatly disappointed me, on a near approach. Like several of the Scotch towns, which owe their beauty to situation, the charm is lost on entering, from the old and irregular appearance of many of the houses, to which a handsome one often unites; and the quantity of fish hung over the doors of the ordinary dwellings, for the purpose of drying, is very disgusting in warm weather. The squalid dirty aspect of the children, take from all the engaging attraction of infancy. Civilisation in the lower class seems here to be almost a century behind, as far as regards necessary comfort; this is the more extraordinary, as there is such a striking superiority of refinement, in language, and courtesy of manner, in the inhabitants of Inverness, which extends to the humblest individual. English is here universally spoken, and in a state of purity and correctness, which renders it perfectly beautiful. It gives a softness to the manners, extremely graceful, which, united with the Highland urbanity of character, at once win upon a stranger. The Gaelic used, I am told, by all the ordinary people, is very comprehensive and powerful. It seems, to my ear, to have great affinity to the Welch.

Despite some mistakes and misjudgements over the years, things have certainly improved!

LOOKING TO THE FUTURE

At the end of the first decade of the twenty-first century, Inverness faces a series of challenges that would have been quite recognisable by our Victorian ancestors or even by our well-meaning post-war planners. In these supposedly more enlightened and certainly more regulated times, we might think that our built heritage is in safer hands. However, there are still threats out there. Viewhill House, gutted by fire, remains the subject of much debate. There is a strong case for renovation, in view of its association with Joseph Mitchell, but architecturally the house was not all that interesting and there is an equally strong case for demolition – as long as the replacement is not another boring block of flats. The redundant bingo hall on the river, on Huntly Street, probably does not have a long-term future – and the area already sports an example of rampant modernism practically next door. The Loch Ness Hotel on Glenurquhart Road is an example of a decaying building on a prime site. Out at Culloden, Stratton Lodge contains an interesting eighteenth-century dower house at its core, but demolition of wretched hotel and restaurant extensions would be required to restore it to anything approaching its former glory. A fire in 2013 makes its survival unlikely.

There are many examples of buildings of merit which are not, as the council managers would say, 'fit for purpose'. They weren't fit for purpose in the twentieth century, so are certainly not fit for purpose in the twenty-first. The railway station is an embarrassment – the adjacent bus station at Farraline Park has been modernised but the opportunity for an integrated public transport complex was missed. The public library at Farraline Park, impossibly located in the middle of the bus station, is in the old Dr Bell's Institution, a nineteenth-century school building with roughly half the floor space specified in national public library standards for library provision in a town the size of Inverness, and without any of the atmosphere or infrastructure of the modern library, or indeed of many Victorian libraries. Fortunately Highland Archives has moved out of Dr Bell's building to an enormous, airy, purpose-built structure at the Bught – such a change from the single airless and windowless former police cell in which they were incarcerated for far too many years.

As the Millennium approached, there was talk – again – of an integrated art gallery, museum, library and exhibition complex in the town centre, but, as usual, nothing came of what seemed, in retrospect, impossibly ambitious plans. More modest plans for a new art gallery and museum got as far as a botched public consultation on the most suitable site, but did not survive the credit crunch. Maybe one day… The current Inverness Museum and Art Gallery has been attractively upgraded and with, at last, a watertight roof, but is far too small for the job it is trying to do. The Bridge Street planners woefully underestimated the library and museum needs, and even when the library moved from Castle Wynd to Farraline Park the space remaining for the museum and art gallery is scandalously inadequate.

Council planners would dearly love to build themselves a new council headquarters, probably in what is now their car park on Glenurquhart Road, since both the nineteenth-century buildings used and their 1970s additions and extensions are now far too small for the Highlands' largest employer. Presumably only the nineteenth-century buildings would survive demolition.

Redundant and unwanted ecclesiastical buildings can only increase in number, and it is not always easy to see how they can be used – we already have enough carpet warehouses in Inverness.

Inverness has a tremendous cultural legacy and a fascinating and interesting history, with many aspects still to be adequately investigated. The history of education in Inverness, never mind the rest of the Highlands, has still to be written, as has the history of the churches and chapels in the town. In former times the complexity of these topics, and the effort which would have been required to unravel all the detail of often quite ephemeral institutions, were serious barriers to further study, but with the advent of modern research techniques, including digital indexing of nineteenth-century newspapers and digitising of rare local history books, these subjects have opened up to researchers and invite study.

Inverness in the nineteenth and twentieth centuries had two or three local newspapers at any one time, all now microfilmed and so much more available to historical researchers than in the past. Some of them are indexed – sufficient to allow leads to be followed up in the ones which are not. Family history specialists have long understood the fantastic riches of information to be found in the local press, but social historians have been slower to make use of these resources. For crime and punishment, disasters, royal visits, weddings and funerals, emigrations and clearances, the laying of foundation stones and the opening of public buildings, school prize givings, declarations of war and peace, obituaries of local worthies, blizzards, accidents and comings of age, the local newspapers await detailed exploitation – not to mention the thousands of Letters to the Editor from thousands of Invernessians with bees in their Highland bonnets.

Inverness continues to grow, with hundreds of houses built or planned every year, even in the depths of recession. But it is still a small Scottish provincial town – it will be decades before the population approaches even 100,000. Inverness is not, and never will be, a 'city', except in the narrow, administrative sense beloved of the narrow, administrative denizens of the council headquarters on Glenurquhart Road. This is nothing to do with whether or not the 'cathedral' has a spire (irrelevant) or the size of the population, but is more to do with the mental geography of its natives.

A feature of recent years has been not only the new, sprawling housing developments, but the continuing decline of the historic town centre, incomprehensibly designated 'Old Town' by the planners. Invernessians used to bemoan the arrival of nationally branded department stores and supermarkets, driving out small shopkeepers, but nowadays they shop with their feet, or wheels, in shopping centres and 'retail parks' on the edge of the town, leaving the town centre to a very few enterprising small businesses and a plethora of charity shops, building societies and mobile phone outlets. Historically, the compact shopping centre was the heart of the town. Most shops were personally supervised by the shopkeepers and their families, giving individual attention to the public. Only the new Eastgate Centre, in its two phases, retains anything of the community atmosphere of the traditional High Street.

Along with these trends, the town centre is typically occupied at weekends by promenading tourists and by hundreds of local revellers, often dressed in impossibly optimistic outfits which then embellish the pages of our local newspapers. At least the tourists now have the benefit of a much better range of eateries than their Victorian predecessors, including some truly outstanding establishments, and the standard of accommodation in hotels, guesthouses and bed and breakfast places has improved at last.

This publication has focused on what has been lost, but a great deal remains. There are many interesting buildings in the town centre, often with interesting stories to tell, which are deserving of more accessible interpretation – existing histories and guides tend to be quite dense, and difficult to acquire. With one or two notable exceptions, the best architecture is to be found in the houses and mansions of the Victorian suburbs. The largest of them have been converted to hotels or care homes, but seem safe from further ravages. Much more could be done to guide visitors around the more attractive parts of the town; often these attractive residences were originally built by the professional and successful merchant classes of Victorian Inverness, by talented and interesting people who would be commemorated by blue plaques elsewhere. With vigilance and imagination, further architectural depredations can be avoided, and our townscape safeguarded for future generations.

FURTHER READING

*

There is an extensive literature on various aspects of the history and development of Inverness; many of the items listed here contain references to other material. Gerald Pollitt's *Historic Inverness* and the Inverness Field Club volume, *The Hub of the Highlands*, both have excellent bibliographies and suggestions for further reading. Books listed here were published in Inverness unless otherwise noted.

Books

Anderson, Isabel Harriet, *Inverness before Railways* (1885, reprinted 1984)

Barron, Evan Macleod, *Inverness and the Macdonalds* (1930)

Barron, Evan Macleod, *Inverness in the Fifteenth Century* (1906)

Barron, Evan Macleod, *Inverness in the Middle Ages* (1907)

Burt, Edmund, *Letters from a Gentleman in the North of Scotland* (London, 1754; reprinted Edinburgh, 1974) 2 vols.

Cook, Joseph, *Joseph Cook's Inverness* (1992)

Delavault, Pierre, *Old Inverness* (1903, reprinted 1967)

Fraser, John, *Reminiscences of Inverness: Its People and Places* (1905)

Fraser-Mackintosh, Charles, *Invernessiana* (1875)

Gaukroger, Jamie and Maclean, Clare, *Inverness: a History and Celebration of the City* (The Francis Frith Collection, 2005)

Glashan, William, *Old Buildings of Inverness* (1978)

Inverness Local History Forum, *Inverness, Our Story: "Mind Thon Time"* (2004)

Inverness Local History Forum, *Inverness, Our Story: "Mind Thon Time"*, Book Two (2007)

Mackintosh, Murdoch, *A History of Inverness* (1939)

Maclean, John, *Reminiscences of a Clachnacuddin Nonagenarian* (1886)

Meldrum, Edward, *Inverness: Local History and Archaeology Guidebook No 4* (1982)

Miller, James, *Inverness* (Edinburgh, 2004)

Newton, Norman S., *Inverness: Highland Town to Millennium City* (Derby, 2003)

Newton, Norman S., *The Life and Times of Inverness* (Edinburgh, 1996)

Pearson, John M., *A Guided Walk round Inverness* (1987)

Pollitt, A. Gerald, *Historic Inverness* (Perth, 1981)

Suter, James, *Memorabilia of Inverness* (1887)

Inverness Field Club Publications

The Dark Ages in the Highlands (1971)

The Hub of the Highlands (1975)

An Inverness Miscellany: No. 1 (1983)

An Inverness Miscellany: No. 2 (1987)

Loch Ness and Thereabouts (1991)

The Middle Ages in the Highlands (1981)

Old Inverness in Pictures (1981)

The Seventeenth Century in the Highlands (1986)

Newspapers

Highland News, 1883–

Inverness Advertiser, 1849–1885*

Inverness Courier, 1817–

Inverness Journal, 1807–1849*

Northern Chronicle, 1881–1969

Scottish Highlander, 1885–1898*

*These titles can be searched by person, subject or keyword in the Newspaper Index of the Am Baile website: *www.ambaile.org.uk*. Searches produce a brief reference to newspaper articles, which can be ordered from Inverness Library, through the Am Baile website. The Reference Room at Inverness Library has microfilm reels of all these titles, and many others.

Periodicals

These journals contain numerous articles relevant to the history of Inverness:

Celtic Magazine, 1876–88

Celtic Monthly, 1892–1917

Transactions of the Gaelic Society of Inverness, 1871–

Transactions of the Inverness Scientific Society and Field Club, 1875–1925

Statistical Accounts

These three inventories of all the parishes in Scotland give excellent summaries of social conditions, industries, education, trade, transport, civic institutions, geography, topography and antiquities. The *First* or *Old Statistical Account* was edited by Sir John Sinclair of Caithness and published in twenty-one volumes between 1790 and 1799. In the 1840s the exercise was repeated as the *New Statistical Account of Scotland*, and a third survey was completed in recent decades. The town of Inverness appears in the submissions for the Parish of Inverness and Bona, and is described as follows, with the date of compilation in brackets:

Old Statistical Account (1791)
New Statistical Account (1835)
Third Statistical Account (1951; revised 1970)

Image Acknowledgements

The numbers refer to the pages on which the images appear.

Reproduced by permission of the Trustees of the National Library of Scotland: 8, 9, 11, 12, 13, 16.

Courtesy of Highland Libraries and Am Baile: 4, 5, 10, 14, 15, 19, 20, 22, 23, 25, 41, 47, 58, 59, 60, 61, 62, 63, 64, 65, 66, 67, 68, 69, 70, 71, 72, 73, 75, 76, 77, 96, 97, 99, 100, 101, 103, 104, 105, 106, 107, 112, 117, 119, 120, 123, 134, 135, 138, 141, 144, 145, 147, 148, 152.

Highland Archives: 39, 115, 208.

Highland Photographic Archive, Inverness Museum and Art Gallery: 34, 37, 72, 95, 98, 102, 103, 108, 109, 110, 111, 113, 114, 115, 116, 117, 137, 138, 141, 142, 143, 149, 150, 151.

Inverness Museum and Art Gallery: 80, 84.

Robert Reid: 111.

Reproduced by kind permission of The Highland Council Planning and Development Service and Am Baile: 139, 140, 146.

Reproduced by kind permission of Mrs Ruth Meldrum: 41.

Index

Note: entries in *italic* are references to illustrations.